DIEHARDS

WHY FANS CARE SO MUCH ABOUT SPORTS

CHIP SCARINZI

Foreword by JOSH PAHIGIAN

Rowe Publishing

ISBN 13: 978-1-939054-48-7
ISBN 10: 1-939054-48-6

Cover photo and author image by Dennis Agatep.

Contact Rowe Publishing for information about special discounts for bulk purchases by phone 785-425-7350 or email info@rowepub.com.

1 3 5 7 9 8 6 4 2

Printed in the United States of America
Published by

Rowe Publishing
www.rowepub.com
Stockton, Kansas

For my loves, Leah, Olivia, and May

... and for diehards everywhere.

CONTENTS

FOREWORD

Why do sports captivate and thrill us? Why do we pour so much of ourselves into the experience of watching adults play the games we loved as children? I've wondered about this for some time.

I still remember the day my curiosity regarding the nature of fandom first arose. My eighth grade history teacher, Mr. Mayotte, pulled me aside one morning to ask what sort of grade I thought I could get in his class if I spent half the time studying that I devoted to baseball. After I muttered a lame reply, he asked *why* I cared so much about the sport. On Fridays, he led us in a game of current affairs trivia. Over the course of several weeks, he had noticed my near-encyclopedic knowledge of the game. I still remember the question that prompted our chat that morning: "Who did the Red Sox trade to get new pitcher Lee Smith?"

As was usually the case when a question from the sports category came up, mine was the first hand in the air.

"The Sox traded two guys for Lee Arthur Smith," I answered. "Calvin Schiraldi and Al Nipper."

Mayotte nodded. "And how are they doing?" he asked.

"Schiraldi's 3-2 with a 4.50 ERA," I sputtered. "Nipper's 1-2 with an ERA in the 2.00s."

There were two things about Shepherd Hill Junior High School that made me eager to climb onto the bus each morning: the promise of baseball practice at the end of the day and the racks of hanging newspapers in the library – the sports pages that I would read through during study hall.

When adults asked what I planned to do when I grew up, I would give the same answer I'd been reciting since attending my first game at Fenway Park in 1982, which just so happened to be a walk-off win in twelve innings, thank you very much Gary Allenson. I was going to play third base for the Boston Red Sox. I was the kid who shoveled snow from the lawn in February so I could throw balls against a strike zone chalked onto the chimney; the kid who ran a fantasy baseball league, figuring out the standings the old-fashioned way, with a calculator and pencil when USA Today ran the league-wide stats on Tuesday; the kid who got an Easter basket full of Topps wax packs every year; the kid who mailed letters to players stuffed with self-addressed and stamped envelopes in hopes of a reply; the kid who used a wooden bat in Little League.

I have been a diehard for as long as I can remember. But that doesn't make me unique. There are millions like me, following different teams in different sports in different countries. But why? Why do we stake so much of our happiness on the bounce of a ball?

My first taste of alcohol came from a champagne bottle my father had been saving since the Red Sox lost to the Reds in the 1975 World Series. I brought the glass to my lips on an October night in 1986, minutes before a groundball would trickle through a first baseman's legs and into my nightmares. Naturally, I blamed my father when the Red Sox fell to the Mets in Game Seven two nights later. He should have known better than to toast victory before the final out.

At some point, of course, my dream of playing in the big leagues yielded to reality's harsh light. A .223 batting average on your J.V. baseball team will do that, especially when you're the guy keeping the team stat book. A couple years later, when it came time to pick a college, proximity to Fenway Park played a primary role in my decision.

I attended every Opening Day at Fenway through my undergrad and grad school years, even after the gut-kick of the 1994 work stoppage had prompted me to send several angry letters to Commissioner Bud Selig, one of which garnered a reply that began, "Dear Josh. Thank you for your letter and for your passion for the game, although I take great exception to your language and use of sarcasm..." I bought a standing room ticket whenever Pedro Martinez was pitching, and on days when those tickets sold out, I handed a folded $20 bill to an usher who would let me pass through his turnstile. I routinely entered the park the minute the gates opened, so I could watch batting practice and interact with the players as they shagged balls. I waited outside the players' parking lot after big wins to cheer my favorites as they headed home.

For four years of grad school I lived close enough to Fenway to walk to games, which I often did with my girlfriend (now wife) Heather beside me. On any given night, we might experience the joy of watching a Shea Hillenbrand homer sail over the left field wall to lift the Red Sox to an 18-inning win over the Tigers, or the indignity of sitting through the latter innings of a 22-1 loss to the dreaded Yankees. To this day, I have never left a ballpark early. There's no clock in baseball, and a comeback is always possible. And besides, I just love being at the ballpark, no matter the score, weather, or time of day.

Sometimes with Heather and other times with friends, I began embarking on baseball trips, exploring the major and minor league offerings along the East Coast. I discovered much to love about the other ballparks too, and realized I had a lot in common with other teams' fans, even if our rooting interests diverged.

Approaching the end of a graduate program in creative writing and with the real world looming, I wrote a wing-and-a-prayer book proposal with a friend and fellow devotee of the game. Finding a publisher seemed as unlikely as witnessing a no-hitter or inside-the-park home run. But amazingly we found an editor willing to front us the cash to visit all thirty big league parks and write a book about an epic baseball adventure shared by two friends. It turned out we had the right idea at the right time. Several new ballparks had just opened and a certain "priceless" credit card commercial had hit the airwaves romanticizing the idea of a summer spent in pursuit of baseball nirvana. *The Ultimate Baseball Road Trip* connected with fellow lovers of the game, and I had found my niche as a baseball travel writer.

So, back to Mr. Mayotte, eighth grade history, and the question of why I care so much. The only answer I could muster then was, "Because I love baseball."

"It's just a game," he replied.

Of course, he was right. But I loved it so damned much. I wished there were some way to transfer to him the joy of a bat in your hands making solid contact with a ball, or of an improbable come-from-behind win for your team, or of watching a center fielder lay out for a diving catch, or of emerging from Kenmore Square and getting that first whiff of sausages, peppers, and onions frying behind the Green Monster. Why did those small miracles appeal to me in a way they evidently didn't to him?

Flash-forward 30 years... and those joys, simple as they may be, still entrance me. But why?

I can't answer this for every fan, but after reading the book you hold in your hands, I am better able to articulate my own reasons for caring so deeply about the game I love and the team I cheer. Baseball has been one of the few constants in my life. Throughout the carefree days of childhood, the uncomfortable years of adolescence, the anxiety of early adulthood, the excitement of starting a married life, the pursuit of making a living, the responsibility of being a father, and every other phase of life, baseball has been there. Other interests have come and gone... ice fishing, what was I thinking? Close friends have scattered to far corners of the country and world. I've held several jobs in addition to my career as a baseball writer. Like most people, I have lived a life of constant adjustment to new realities and new responsibilities. But the promise of tomorrow's game or of Opening Day has always been present, carrying me through the darkest of nights and coldest of winters. My identity as "baseball lover" has remained. Baseball is my anchor amid life's sea of uncertainty.

Through this fine book – that is as lively and humorous as it is well researched and insightful – Chip Scarinzi has brought me to a deeper understanding of my own obsession. The author does a remarkable job deconstructing the excitement, joy, frustration, heartbreak, and range of other emotions sports bring into our lives. Reading this book will bring you closer to being able to put to words the feelings in your own heart for the team(s) you love. The author deftly weaves accounts of his own first-hand experiences as fan with those of other fanatics, while incorporating the insight gleaned from experts in anthropology, sociology, psychology, neuroscience, religion and other fields to explore and analyze sports' hold over us. I hope you enjoy this richly layered book as much as I did. And I hope you continue to find in the experience of rooting for your team(s) whatever it is that sports offer you.

Josh Pahigian
Author of *The Ultimate Baseball Road Trip* and
101 Baseball Places to See Before You Strike Out

1

"WHAT IS HAPPENING IN OAKLAND?"

Even now, it's hard to describe the feeling.

At first, it was suffocating. The sense of inevitability. Overwhelming disappointment. Helplessness. We stood shoulder-to-shoulder in a light rain that seemed to drag the Oakland Athletics' season with it down the drain. Earlier in the evening, the crowd clung to the faint pulse of its team's shrinking chances of victory. They desperately wanted to believe their team had a shot at sneaking past the visiting Detroit Tigers even while trailing deep in the game. While not ideal, a one-run deficit in the eighth inning of this win-or-go-home playoff battle was hardly insurmountable. Now, just a few minutes later, a late tally off of rookie southpaw Sean Doolittle sent the A's hopes – and everyone looking on from the outskirts of Downtown Oakland – reeling.

Doolittle, a highly touted prospect whose star had faded with injuries, reached the sport's pinnacle with a midseason call-up. His journey to this American League Divisional Series mound, however, was an unusual one. Beset by injuries, the Athletics' first baseman of the future faced long odds of remaining healthy enough to secure a steady job at his original position. Coming to grips with the necessity of a position change, Doolittle worked with his minor league instructors to reinvent himself as

1

a pitcher in the low minors. Doolittle had pitched in college, but this was a last-ditch effort to salvage a dying big league dream. The transformation worked just about as well as anyone could have predicted: just 25 minor league innings later, Doolittle stood on a big league mound in early June for his debut and promptly struck out three of the four batters he faced. Armed with a deadly fastball and developing secondary pitches, he mowed down American League batters for four months and proved to be downright filthy against lefties. Here in the eighth inning and under the bright lights of October baseball, however, the Cinderella story had run out of steam and into some tough luck. The script unfolded simply enough: a base hit followed by a sacrifice bunt, which set the stage for a backbreaking run-scoring single. Deflated diehards sank deep into their seats, now slick and chilled with droplets of rain. The mood shifted from hopeful to miserable to reflective. *If it all ends tonight, it sure has been a hell of a run ...*

The Athletics were staring down elimination and facing another disappointing October finish. Jose Valverde, the Tigers' eccentric closer, took a final warm-up toss and finished his ritual calisthenics routine by hopping, skipping, and jumping his way to the mound. Nothing gets under your skin more as a fan than when an opposing player showboats on his way out to the field. Together, bleary-eyed and voiceless, we hoped our team could shock the world and knock Valverde down a couple of pegs. As gratifying as that outcome might be for the home crowd, it felt like a pipe dream at this late stage of the game. All that separated the Tigers from playing on into the next round were three pesky outs.

We screamed and we yelled. We prayed to God. We prayed to the Baseball Gods.

Josh Reddick began the ninth inning with a base hit to right field as a murmur began to resonate from every corner of the ballpark. No lead was safe against these A's. After all, this team had stolen 14 games in their final at-bat during the regular season and captured the American League West division title from the high-octane Texas Rangers on the season's final day. We were all hoping that the Boys from the Bay could do it one more time.

We didn't have to wait long for the tide to begin turning. Josh Donaldson nearly tied the game with a first-pitch liner off the top of the wall in left-center, sending Reddick to third and bringing the winning run to the plate with no outs.

Like Doolittle, Donaldson had also taken a winding path to the big leagues. Buried behind other options as a minor league catcher, the A's thrust the slow-to-develop backstop into the role of full-time third baseman at the start of the season – not by choice, but rather, out of necessity when promising expected starter Scott Sizemore suffered a season-ending knee injury during the first and only action that he would see in spring training. Sizemore's emergency understudy battled to learn a new position on the job, and struggled mightily at the plate. Losing patience with Donaldson's development during his first stint as an everyday third baseman, the team sent him packing for Triple-A Sacramento with a late-April demotion. Away from the spotlight, something clicked. He hit. He made routine plays at third base. He made spectacular plays at third base. When the big league club came calling after yet another injury, this time to veteran fill-in Brandon Inge, Donaldson grabbed his second chance and never let go. Into the playoffs, Donaldson appeared to have found his way both with the bat and at the hot corner.

Waves of noise crashed over a frenzied capacity crowd of more than 36,000 long-suffering fans. The excitement was palpable. With one swing of the bat, Josh Donaldson had cemented his legacy as a fan favorite in Oakland. The

A's were exorcising the demons of past shortcomings and fans now had one more reason to believe that this squad was different.

And they were.

The Athletics were wholly inadequate when contrasted with tonight's opponents. Detroit marched into Oakland a veritable all-star team featuring future Hall of Famers at the corners and patrolling the pitcher's mound. How can you contain Triple Crown-winner Miguel Cabrera and powerful first baseman Prince Fielder? How can you survive a short series against perennial Cy Young candidates Justin Verlander and Max Scherzer? These Tigers were loaded. In stark contrast on the other side of the field, the Athletics cobbled together a squad featuring converted outfielders playing the infield, catchers holding down infield positions, and platoons at nearly every spot on the field. Where were the superstars? Where were the household names?

There were none, and if you ask A's fans, most prefer it this way. The A's – their over-achieving A's – toil in anonymity, but just keep winning.

Donaldson had just sent his stock soaring into the chilly October air, and moments later, it was Seth Smith's turn to become a legend – if only for the night. The third batter of the inning ensured that there would be more baseball in Oakland on a wet, cold evening by following Donaldson's shot with a gapper of his own. Both runners scored to tie the game, and the league's best story of the 2012 season penned the latest unbelievable chapter of their tale while Smith pumped his fist and screamed out in joy at second base.

I can only imagine the scene in the press box as dozens of scribes and storytellers ripped their game reports to shreds and settled in for a long night. "A's Eliminated by Mighty Tigers as Offense Goes Quiet" no longer fit the moment, regardless of how it might end. Select all, delete, and a fresh pot of coffee brewing for good measure. This night, October 10, 2012, was shaping up to be a long one. Two batters later, hope began to slip away again. Smith remained tethered to second base with his hands on his hips after two quick outs. *At least we still have a shot in extras*, the collective fan base rationalized. The momentum, even if lessened, still resided with the home nine. Refusing to let up and admit defeat, fans screamed and shouted, jumped and gyrated. Is it even possible to will a team to win? We thought so. Everyone wanted to contribute, at least in a small way, to bringing a win to Oakland as the team's igniter and dependable leadoff man stepped to the plate.

At this stage of his career, journeyman veteran Coco Crisp always seemed to bounce back and forth between both the trading block and the front lines of the A's most magical moments. This was about to become the latest example of the latter.

On the first offering from Valverde, Crisp pushed a groundball through the hole on the right side to send the winning run home and drive the crowd into a euphoric state of pure joy and fantastical elation. "What is happening in Oakland?" – a refrain popularized by the Athletics' broadcast team throughout this magical season – rang out from the broadcast booth one more time. The game was over. The good guys had won. And 36,000 jubilant fans floated off into outer space.

While Crisp and his teammates celebrated the victory as if it were the last of the season – and, as it turns out, it was – we did the same in the stands. Friends shared high-fives and strangers embraced. The stadium, antiquated and outdated, rumbled as if the Earth was shaking. For all we knew, it was. After all, it had rained in the middle innings and no one dared run for cover. We were falling in love all over again – with a team, a city, a story. More than that, we were falling in love with an overwhelming emotional sensation. It was a strange and indescribable reaction to the events unfolding on the field below, but you could feel it percolate from section to section and ricochet off the concrete steps and the tarps of Mount Davis, high above the action. Each of us, huddled together in the concrete oval, had a stake in the blockbuster movie that just came to a magical end on perfectly cut grass, and a gritty dirt infield.

What were we even doing there? The Athletics had no business being in the playoffs in the first place, and neither did the fans who celebrated this win as if it were their own. Why do these games even matter to us as much as they do? All I know is that on this night, I didn't want to be anywhere else and I most certainly did not intend to make a hasty exit. I stayed for another hour after the final pitch, and wandered the concourse until every fan had left the building and left me alone with my thoughts and my equally elated companion for the game. Peering out from beyond the outfield wall, stadium workers hummed along like tiny bees behind vacuums and brooms. *This must be what Billy Beane does after the park clears out*, we decided. Billy Beane, the team's general manager and mad scientist, had put the pieces of this winning ball club in place on a shoestring budget. The talk radio blowhards questioned his every move during the offseason, which is always a great time for paper champions to rule the day while actual champions fly under the radar. Beane caused an uncomfortable amount of consternation by toiling away all winter trading his most talented players and filling holes with unknowns. *There is no way this team can compete*, they yelled confidently through the radio. *The Athletics will lose 100 games*, the experts philosophized. Surpassing expectations in such dramatic fashion perhaps

6

made tonight's victory that much sweeter. In a few short weeks, the league would honor this maniac as its Executive of the Year.

Echoes of that night's magic – oh, that beautiful, deafening sound! – still rang in my ears as the evening quieted. I stayed for as long as I could, soaking in every element of a perfect night before leaving the park behind – my second home, my Cathedral – for a final time in 2012.

Less than 24 hours later, the high-powered Detroit Tigers made quick work of the Athletics behind all-world ace Justin Verlander, as the offense did indeed go quietly into the night. 6-0. Season over. The game served as an anti-climactic letdown that sent 25 teammates in 25 different directions for the long, cold offseason. The A's tale, as it turned out, was a beautifully crafted short story with an abrupt ending. The Tigers had volumes to write as they continued toward a World Series berth, where they would ultimately fall just short of the grand prize.

The experience of October 10 gnawed at me all winter. I wanted it, whatever it was, again and again. I felt the need to describe it, with unapologetic futility, to everyone I came across during the winter chill. In the cruelest of twists, the cross-bay rival San Francisco Giants would motor down Market Street in celebration of their second title in three years a few short weeks after the A's magic ran dry. I tried to trick myself into believing that the A's had already won the World Series on Coco's base knock three weeks earlier. All of this – the games that followed between other teams and this gratuitous showcase of excess by the neighboring Giants – was merely an exhibition. In the hearts of the diehards, the Oakland Athletics were champions.

Sometime between November and April, the familiar sounds of bat cracks and mitt pops returned as they always do. That winter, I began to understand why I cared so much about sports and why outcomes of games I have no control over (or do I?) mattered to me. I have struggled mightily to put it into words, but that one night inside the O.co Coliseum changed forever my DNA as a fan of baseball. A momentary brush with greatness shared among an exclusive group lucky enough to have been "chosen" by the Baseball Gods to be present for something spectacular. Was it merely the excitement of a game-winning hit? No, surely it was more than that. A game-winning hit to stave off elimination for another day. A game-winning hit that followed a comeback from a two-run deficit to pull victory from the jaws of defeat. A game-winning hit after the gut-punch of watching it all slip away late in the game, before the most glorious comeback this side of San Francisco Bay. Is there a formula for unadulterated euphoria? For a transcendent religious experience? If there is, I must have found it. That night, a game-winning hit forever linked a team to 36,000 supporters braving the rain and an eight-inning heartbreak because of a moment – a feeling – that many will undoubtedly spend the rest of their lives trying to find again.

Dr. Daniel Wann, a psychology professor at Murray State University and one of the foremost experts on the psychology of sports fans, has studied this kind of human reaction to athletic competition for more than 30 years. In 1995, Wann authored a study in the *Journal of Sport and Social Issues* titled, "Preliminary Validation of the Sport Fan Motivation Scale," that introduced the idea of quantifying and confirming fandom. He sought validation for that squishy, unsubstantiated experience hundreds of millions of people around the world share. Thus, the Sport Fan Motivation Scale was born. Further corroborated by Wann and a pair of his contemporaries in a 1999 *Journal of Sport Behavior* follow-up study, the scale leverages findings from survey data measuring eight different motives of sports fans. These motives consist of eustress (craving the adrenaline rush of sport), self-esteem, escape, entertainment, economics, aesthetics, group affiliation, and family. While his research settled on several conclusions, I found one outcome particularly intriguing as I began studying the psychology of sports fans. Wann determined that individuals driven by one or more of six of these motives tend to view themselves as fans of sport. Wait, I thought there were eight motives, you might ask. Among the eight, Wann found that family and economic motivations failed to connect people with fandom. Keeping an eye on monetary investments (in other words, you've placed bets on the outcome) or using a game as an excuse for a family outing live outside of the realm of diehard sports fandom. In these instances, the game is simply a means to an end, a convenient mechanism for enjoying other pursuits in life. However, according to Wann, fans flocking to the turnstiles for any one of the other six motivations do identify consistently as sports fans. If you consider yourself a sports fan, take a quick look at each of these terms and see if they match up with your own motivations.

Fans motivated by eustress, which I'll admit required a visit to Webster's Dictionary, live for the excitement and anxiety that sport delivers. It also keeps them coming back for more. The measure of self-esteem is the standard "basking in reflective glory" scenario: you are living vicariously through your sports heroes. Their success is your success. Escape and entertainment require minimal explanation. We might need to start from the beginning if an explanation is required for why a three-hour break from the stresses and responsibilities of reality might be pleasing. Or why some fans might find the competitive aspect of sports appealing.

That leaves group affiliation and aesthetics. Most people enjoy the company of others and for many fans, sports can satisfy the need to affiliate with other people.

The aesthetic appeal of athletics is a bit cerebral – this is where we get into the appreciation some feel for the art form of sports. As I write this, my wife is somewhere rolling her eyes. Aesthetics as a motivator covers fans who crave athletic excellence, while also leaving room for the romantics among us who believe that these games are just so darn beautiful. You know the type. They're seduced by the look of a freshly cut lawn and the sound of the ball popping in a well-worn mitt. They appreciate the smell of a creaky old ballpark that has seen one too many spilled beers and enough peanut shells to last a lifetime. Does that sound familiar? I'm sure a few people out there need only look in the mirror.

This all brings me back to Coco Crisp and that magical night in Oakland where I concluded that baseball is awesome and I wanted to live forever inside the O.co Coliseum. The event – not only the game-winning hit, but also the event in its entirety with everything on the line – triggered for me several of Wann's identified motivations. Diehard baseball fandom attached itself to me many years earlier in my youth. Sports have maintained a steady pull on me throughout my life. The pleasure felt that evening, however, positively validated the emotional investment I had made in this scraggly bunch of throwbacks few believed in before the season began.

"Anybody you talk to who is a diehard fan of a team has those types of memories. Some of the most powerful memories we have are attached to some type of emotion, and what's more emotional than a win-or-go-home scenario for a team that you're a diehard fan of?" Wann asked me a couple years later as I retold the story from a memory as vivid and clear as if the game had just happened. Then, to underscore his point, he shared a similar moment with me from his own experience as a diehard fan of both the Chicago Cubs and Kansas City Royals. "I can remember watching Ryne Sandberg hit two home runs in 1984, which basically propelled the Cubs to the playoffs for the first time in my lifetime. You're talking about something that was 30 years ago and I can remember where I was sitting, I can remember the carpet, I can remember what I was eating. And similarly, I can remember when they lost and blew a two-games-to-none lead in the playoffs that year, and my Royals lost to the Tigers [in the American League Championship Series that year]. God, I hate the Tigers.

"There are so many things that go on within the realm of sports fandom," he continued. "And here's my point: it's not just that it's a huge part of who we are – it is. It's not just that we can't really control the outcome – that's a part of it, that's not just it. It's not just that it's a crazy emotional rollercoaster. It is, but that's not [all that it is]. It's the fact that it's a social activity and anything you do that you share with others, and in this case 45,000 others, is going to amp up the intensity. It's a euphoric event that you're sharing with 45,000 of your best friends. Granted, you don't know the names of 44,995 of them, but they're still your best friends. It's a social activity."

Thanks to Coco Crisp, the 2012 Oakland Athletics and the horde of revelers with whom I spent one incredible evening, I stumbled upon what I was searching for every time I entered a ballpark. I just don't know where or when it will happen again, and that is why I keep coming back. If you are a fan, it might be what brings you back too.

———

This is probably a good time to share that I am, in fact, a lifelong, diehard Philadelphia Phillies fan. As a child of the 1980s in suburban New Jersey, I aligned with the much-maligned Philadelphia franchise while my friends scattered their allegiances among the more successful

New York teams. The New York Mets were enjoying new-found relevance following their second World Series title in 1986. Further north in the Bronx, a decade-long slumber from playoff contention did little to take the shine off a storied New York Yankees franchise among my inner circle of budding baseball nerds. We were little historians in those days, soaking up as much knowledge about our chosen squads as possible.

I have a soft spot for underdogs, and in my endless obsession with baseball history, it did not take long for me to realize I had selected the ultimate underdog as my team of choice. The Phillies stand alone as the losingest franchise in sports history, having crested the dubious milestone of 10,000 losses during the summer of 2007. No matter; they were my team and I loved them. I studied roster moves and researched their history. I scratched out real-time hitting and pitching statistics on note cards while listening to the soothing voices of Harry Kalas and Richie Ashburn call games deep into the night. In 1993, I cried when Joe Carter ended the Phillies miracle run at the World Series with a series-clinching homerun. I would finally experience that moment of glory myself 15 years later, but from afar in a small one-bedroom apartment in San Francisco.

My fascination with baseball history led me, some 25 years later, to the cement and steel of the Oakland Coliseum. Before I made it inside the tarp-covered multi-sport stadium that rests along Highway 880 on the outskirts of Oakland, I studied diligently from afar. When I am in a position to defend my fandom – why a Phillies fan from New Jersey deserves permission to root with similar fervor for a second team in the same sport – I tend to gravitate toward the same story. That story always begins the same way. A deep breath, and then I unfurl an enthusiastic tale about the surprising discovery made by a studious Philadelphia sports history buff in the mid-1980s: the Oakland Athletics found their way to the West Coast by way of Philadelphia. This second team was, in many ways, the first team in the hearts of Philadelphians of their era. First in every other aspect of the game short of being the literal first team in town. For several years, the Philadelphia Athletics dominated the fledgling American League while their cross-town National League counter-parts bounced along the bottom in those early years of professional ball. Capturing six League pennants and three World Championships between 1902 and 1914 cemented the Athletics as a real dynasty, but their run of excellence in Philadelphia would be brief. Several years of struggle followed the team's success. In 1954, the Athletics played their final season in Philadelphia and then set out on their nomadic journey to the Bay Area, with a 12-year pit stop through Kansas City.

My exposure to the Oakland Athletics was fleeting during the early years of my baseball love affair. I read the box scores in my local paper and memorized baseball card stats as though I was preparing for an exam. The great fortune of the late 1980s is that I'd only need to wait until playoff time to catch a glimpse of these ball players from the Wild West. These larger-than-life megastars bashed their way to three consecutive World Series appearances and one World Championship. To a child, the Bash Brothers – Mark McGwire and Jose Canseco – looked like superheroes, flicking tiny white orbs into orbit with tooth-picks. Rickey Henderson, the "Man of Steal," tormented opposing pitchers with his otherworldly speed like no one I had seen before. The Phillies were my team. I loved my perennial last-place losers. The A's were an elicit fantasy of baseball excess. They were bigger, stronger, faster … hell, even the weather looked more pleasant in sunny California.

So then, relocating to the Bay Area in the mid-2000s put me squarely in the catbird seat to become more intimately acquainted with the Oakland Athletics. And while the cast of characters had changed from those glory years of my childhood, my fascination with the green and gold remained, even if marred by the slightest twinge of guilt. Will people call into question my lifelong support of the Phillies if I choose to don an A's cap? Will others question the depth of my loyalty to the Athletics when they learn I only started attending games at the Coliseum in 2008? How do I reconcile years of Phillies loyalty with the fact that I now divert at least half of my attention to another team in another league? I am always on edge, and armed with my lengthy tale to solidify my standing among diehards on both coasts.

"Research shows that sports fans are fans of multiple teams, and oftentimes multiple teams in the same sport. So if you're going to be a Phillies fan and an A's fan, from a psychological perspective, that's a wonderfully healthy thing to do," said Wann, much to my relief. "This year [2014], I love that those are your two teams because this year is a perfect case in point. If you were only a Phillies fan, what kind of year are you having? But because you've got this additional option, that gives you a second chance at a good season. Psychologically, it's a really smart strategy to take and a lot of fans do it." Worth noting here that, to answer Wann's question, I would be having a terrible year. At the time of our conversation, my bottom-dwelling Phillies had been grappling with the reality of an aging core of veterans and a limited pool of adequate replacement talent in its barren minor league system. For Phillies fans, the harsh reality is that our five-year window of glory – the Golden Age of Baseball in Philadelphia – had closed.

In any case, those around me have had primo seats to witness my progression from an interested observer to

dyed-in-the-wool diehard over a period of seasons. What
started with a single pleasant afternoon affair that felt
more like an anthropological study of West Coast baseball – the hometown nine were taking on their cross-bay
rivals, the San Francisco Giants, after all – escalated into
a towel-waving, stranger-hugging outpouring of passion
and emotion a few short years later. Why did this happen?
What fueled this incredible outward response? So many
questions, and the most puzzling of all is whether it is all
just a big waste of time and energy. Does it matter when
the outpouring of love and adoration by fans is seldom, if
ever, reciprocated? I hope so, and I have learned that I'm
not alone in my optimism.

2
FAITH AND FANATICISM

Ask Father Jim Greanias about October 2, 2008, and he will graciously oblige. That was the day that the Greek Orthodox priest blessed the Chicago Cubs dugout prior to Game One of the 2008 National League Divisional Series at the behest of Cubs President Crane Kenney. Cubs fans also remember it as the day that the visiting Los Angeles Dodgers laid waste to their beloved Cubbies on the way to a three-game sweep and an early playoff ouster for the Northsiders.

Blessing a playing field and praying for player safety is a standard spiritual exercise. For spooked Cubs fans catching a glimpse of the act, it conjured something different. This was the stuff of nightmares. Scenes from blockbuster horror flicks featuring priests ridding the world of demons with chants and holy water. *The power of Christ compels you!* What was this outlandish display underway on the hallowed grounds of Wrigley Field? It's one thing for fans to believe in superstition – that the Cubs are cursed – but attempting to rid those cursed demons with a priest's blessing? Had the Cubs organization begun to believe, like their fans, that such a thing could exist? What an outrage!

"I think the disappointment for me was in Crane Kenney because he called me and said, 'I'm a Catholic, and I believe in this,'" Greanias said. "The following January at the annual Cubs Convention, Kenney stood up and said,

'Wow, wasn't that the stupidest thing I've ever done.' Since when is an act of faith something stupid?"

You can ask him about that day, and he will tell you everything he can recall about his pre-game blessing and the heartbreaking loss that followed. Just another Cubbie Occurrence – more evidence that the lovable losers at Wrigley remain under a spell cast many years prior by a disgruntled fan that happened to own a goat. Oh, that hated goat! Fans know that Bill Sianis, owner of Chicago's Billy Goat Tavern & Grill, cast an ironclad hex on the club in 1945. Legend has it that the fabled Curse of the Billy Goat, as it'll be known until the Cubs win the season's final game, occurred when ushers booted the tavern owner's mascot goat from the ballpark during the fourth game of the World Series against the Detroit Tigers. The goat, brought to the game as a promotional gimmick, would not receive a hospitable welcome in Wrigley Field box seats during this title run. Steamed by this egregious affront by the Cubs organization – the goat had a perfectly good ticket! – Bill cast a spell on the Friendly Confines and the Tigers clinched the sport's top prize in seven games. Real or imagined, it is just as easy to pin the club's failures on a stupid goat today as it was back then.

"It bothered me as a priest. Instead of standing up and saying, 'You know what, as an act of personal faith I wanted the team to be blessed. [This was] the personal expression of my own personal faith; I invited the priest to come and bless the field, and that's all it was,'" Greanias said. "I think anyone who would have said they did this out of an expression of faith they [fans] would accept that. 'I wasn't trying to chase away goats; it was my way of expressing faith.'"

Do not dwell for too long on the unfortunate combination of Greanias' modern day blessing, mid-century hocus-pocus and the Cubs playoff meltdown – a spooky coincidence. You may miss a much more important date in the life of the affable and friendly man of faith. Even worse, you will surely miss the better story of a true Cubs diehard.

The story begins on August 19, 1969. On a pleasant Tuesday in the Windy City, locals awoke to a welcomed reprieve from the unbearable summertime heat of Chicago. While most folks toiled away at the work-a-day grind, 37,514 lucky souls crossed the street at West Addison and North Sheffield to catch late-summer baseball. For Cubs fans, it was shaping up to be a season to remember at Wrigley Field: home of the runaway leaders of the National League East. Forget for a moment that this season, like so many before it, was destined for failure. After all, we have already established in this chapter that the Cubs are cursed – the highest reaches of success are not permitted under such conditions. Historians remember 1969 for the historic late-season surge of the eventual World Series Champion "Miracle Mets," which tells you all you need to know about the Cubs' fate. There would be no parade in Chicago in the fall of '69 thanks to a free-fall in the season's final 40 contests and the aforementioned run of New York's less celebrated second squad. However, none of that matters on this day because the barnstorming Chicago Cubs were at the top of their game, and hopes were as high as the sun for the first pitch at 1:30 p.m. The dark days ahead mattered little to an eight-year-old named Jimmy Greanias from Evergreen Park on Chicago's south side, whose life changed forever at his first ballgame inside that quaint little park off Addison and Sheffield.

As his uncle raced along Lake Shore, Jimmy peered out the window at the city passing by on one side and miles upon miles of beaches on the other. Passing Soldier Field, home of the Chicago Bears, and the ruins of the 1893 World's Fair, Jimmy could hear chimes in the distance as the clock struck 11 on that bright, sunny morning. Crossing Belmont, Jimmy looked for signs of historical significance and tradition. After all, the history of his beloved Cubs was brimming with storied moments, both good and bad, as one of the senior circuit's oldest franchises. Of course, as a boy of eight, he had one thing in mind. The mission of the moment consisted of catching a glimpse of the famed statue honoring Captain Philip Sheridan perched triumphantly atop a horse, resting at the corner of Belmont and Lake Shore. Do not mistake young Jimmy for a burgeoning history buff hoping to spot his favorite Civil War hero. Rather, he was looking for something different, something to make his parents blush: colors of the visiting Atlanta Braves painted on the horse's testicles. In accordance with tradition, visiting team rookies suffer hazing rituals on the ride to Wrigley Field. Grizzled vets would chauffeur each gullible newbie off the team bus and force the kids to announce their club's arrival to the Windy City with brush, paint, and more than a few cherry red cheeks. You can call it an initiation to the big leagues, of sorts. "Honoring" the good Captain before an audience of chortling teammates rests among the rites of passage that wide-eyed newcomers must endure as part of the mythology of locker room culture. For Jimmy, it's confirmation of his belief in the unseen. Confirmation that the wild things he had read about the life of a ballplayer are real. Yes, Jimmy. *The rookies in fact, do paint the horse's genitals. Now can we move on?*

Slowing down, the rhythmic beat of the left turn signal indicated that the family's pilgrimage from 20 miles south was coming to its end. A few blocks down Addison toward Wrigley Field, Jimmy started hearing the familiar sounds of baseball in Chicago that he had read about in newspapers or seen briefly in local news coverage of his beloved Cubs. *Programs! Get yer programs here!*

Approaching on foot, he could hear the upbeat melody of a brass quartet emanating from just up the road, and he could almost smell the hot dogs and stale beer. Then suddenly, two blocks short of their destination, there it was. Whoa. I can't believe I'm here. He had seen Wrigley Field hundreds of times on his little black and white TV, but this was different. The moment felt different in every way imaginable. Wrigley Field, bustling with activity just prior to the first pitch of the game, stood tall at the corner of Addison and Sheffield. Affixed to its front, a brilliant red marquee proudly proclaimed the brick, mortar, and steel of the surrounding exterior as the unmistakable "Home of the Chicago Cubs." Peering down Clark Street along his new home away from home, Jimmy could see the bleachers rising over the sidewalk and nearly into the street. High above, the glorious green scoreboard – until that moment, shades of white and grey burned into his mind having caught a glimpse only on TV – stretched to the heavens above. The wondrous marvel, adorned with vertically ranked flags at its tip-top representing each divisional foe, reported the Cubs' standing among their National League competitors during these dog days of summer. With an eight-game lead over the New York Mets, the Cubs were at the top of the flagpole, and on top of the world.

Entering the dark and narrow corridors that compose the main arteries of Wrigley Field, Jimmy descended a short flight of stairs and headed into the path toward the field for the first time. Ascending another short flight of stairs – fans step down just to climb back up to field level, which is just another lovable quirk of the old ballpark – Heaven on Earth came into view before him. The bright blues and reds of the home uniform, a perfectly manicured outfield lawn and groundskeepers watering and raking the burnt orange infield to perfection all in front of him as if a gift from God. Everything around him in that cozy ballpark felt at once so familiar, and at the same time, like nothing he had ever seen before. He knew every contour of the field. He appreciated the peculiarity of how each foul line bent slightly as they reached into the outfield at the old yard. He marveled at how the ivy traced its path along the unforgiving brick wall just beneath the bleacher bums calling out for attention, emboldened by a couple ice-cold Old Style beers on a lazy weekday afternoon.

He took it all in and then settled into his seat, perched a mere four rows behind his Midway Heroes nestled in the dugout just below. While his uncle went back into the concourse on the hunt for a Chicago dog and a bag of peanuts, Jimmy started taking mental notes as the larger-than-life superstars jogged by casually. *Mr. Santo! Mr. Santo! You're my favorite player.* Santo tilted his head and sent a nonchalant wave and maybe a little chuckle toward the chubby, over-exuberant Greek kid exploding with excitement in the first few rows. *There's Ernie Banks!*

Indeed, there was the old man, pounding the palm of his first baseman's mitt. Time had taken its toll on the legend's range, and his defensive skills began to wane, the inevitable effects of age robbing him of the agility and quickness required of the middle infield positions he had once patrolled. The future Hall of Famer had earned his final All-Star Game nod just a month earlier despite the gradual decline of his enormous talents. The man who had famously coined the phrase, "Let's play two!" in reference to his love for playing the game, was running short on games left to play. Yes, the 1969 All-Star Game sure had the feel of a farewell tour for the likable Ernie Banks, who would stick around two more years before calling it quits. Banks, a Cub for life, immortalized in bronze – both at the entrance to Wrigley Field and in the fabled halls of Cooperstown. Jimmy could not take his eyes off the Chicago legend.

Bleacher bums stirred all at once as hoots and hollers began emanating from just above the ivy-covered left field wall. The scene, perhaps puzzling to the casual observer, served as further confirmation that the traditions Jimmy had heard about were alive and well at Wrigley Field. So they screamed and yelled, and they called out names. *Haaands! Haaands! Selmaaa! Selmaaa!* On cue, Cubs pitchers Bill Hands and Dick Selma popped up from the bullpen and waved towels out toward the bleachers to thunderous applause. Mission accomplished. It was all part of the experience inside Wrigley Field.

The game itself had a playoff atmosphere to it – at least, as much as you might expect on a Tuesday afternoon in August. The Braves had lost four of five games and played with the sense of urgency typical of teams clinging to faint playoff hopes. For the hometown Cubs, these games represented daily opportunities to fine-tune their well-oiled machine and strengthen their stranglehold on a National League pennant that had eluded them since 1945. Perhaps because historians remember this game, no. 122 on the schedule, for another reason, it's easy to forget that six future Hall of Famers suited up and went to battle between the white lines – three on each side.

Ken Holtzman, a 23-year-old just coming into his own on the mound, went to work in the first inning and sent the Braves down in order with a groundout and a couple lazy flies to right field. Holtzman's mastery of the Braves lineup would be a recurring theme on this day as young Jimmy sat just above the Cubs dugout and watched the zeros pile up on the scoreboard. Following a couple base knocks to the left side, Jimmy squealed with joy as his hero Ron Santo launched a fly ball beyond the walls of Wrigley Field to put the Cubs on top by three. The Cubs had spotted Holtzman three first inning runs to provide all the support he would need – a good thing too because it was all he would get.

The Braves eight-hole hitter worked a walk in the third, but he would not advance further as Holtzman sent the next two batters down in order. The kid was dealing and making quick work of a potent lineup, and it would continue this way as the game progressed. The outs piled up, and the sun shifted from east to west in the sky. A murmur began to percolate throughout the crowd. *Hey friend, I think we're seeing something special right now.* Entering the seventh inning, Holtzman had held the mighty Braves lineup to two harmless walks. Every well-placed pitch elicited a wild frenzy of applause from the crowd. He was pitching a no-hitter.

That almost changed in the top of the seventh, but a play that left many scratching their heads preserved Holtzman's place in history. Hank Aaron, having another MVP-caliber season (he would finish third in the voting), caught an offering from Holtzman and sent it out to the wall in left. Aaron's blast put an end to the pitcher's no-hit bid after six near-perfect innings. Only it didn't.

"I still remember seeing Billy Williams standing at the wall in left field catching Hank Aaron's fly ball that some-how came back into the stadium," Greanias, the little boy in the fourth row, recalled some 45 years later. Aaron's ball, a surefire homerun if there ever was one, fooled everyone in the stadium – even Williams. Chicago's famous winds knocked Aaron's blast down just as it appeared destined for the bleachers. On its descent, the ball presented the optical illusion of appearing to clear the fence and reenter the playing field, where it landed safely in the webbing of Williams' glove to preserve the no-hitter for the moment. Nine batters later, Holtzman made history. "The whole summer was unbelievable in Chicago because the city was in euphoria over the Cubs. Then I go to my first game, and I see a no-hitter, and I was like, 'whoa.'"

Euphoria. He stopped short of calling it a religious experience. As a man of faith, Greanias has first-hand knowledge of the elements of a true religious experience. In sports, we often categorize special moments as such. So then, to determine whether or not it's possible to have an actual religious experience at a sporting event, we need to better understand what that even means in the first place.

"I think it's [religious experiences] the realization of the mystery occurring before you. In the Orthodox Church, the Holy Communion – the bread and wine – actually becomes the body and blood of Christ. As the Lord said in scripture, 'This is my body, this is my blood.' He didn't say, 'this is like my body, this is like my blood.' When that transfiguration occurs, there's a point in the liturgy when a priest lifts up the host, the bread, which is now the body of Christ. There's always a sense of trembling because you're realizing something above and beyond yourself that you can't understand," Greanias explained. "Perhaps in sports, when your team wins and it doesn't happen that often, you don't know how to react. You don't know what to do, you've seen something that gives you an ultimate joy that you otherwise wouldn't understand. Religion is helping you understand your place in the world, but I think sports give you a chance to be a part of something."

Greanias believes that within these subtleties exists the fundamental difference between sensations that are possible within the confines of the ballpark and those when believers feel closest to God. "It's kind of like when something really makes you laugh and you feel like you're going to pass out. That moment somehow connects with you and you just lose all sense of decorum or, I guess, all sense of constraints in this world. You really are living in the moment and I think that's where the joy comes from," he said while describing his own experience with sports euphoria. "You laugh that hard rarely, and when you do, you have no control over your body and you have no control of anything else except for the ability to just smile and shout or just to smile and laugh and feel giddy.

"And that's different than a religious euphoria. I think the one [associated with sports] is more explosive and the other is more a sense of being in awe. I'm in awe when I lift the host up, and it's more of a fear – not afraid – but a fear where you don't want to just release a lot of emotions."

Contrasted with faith, while live sporting events may spark similar emotional responses to religious euphoria, one fundamental difference, in Greanias' view, makes the comparison null and void. For centuries, believers and nonbelievers have debated and agreed to disagree about the core schism between the two: a fundamental belief or disbelief, in an unseen higher power. A religious experience serves as a reward, of sorts, for those who blindly follow an invisible leader. And just try explaining it when it occurs. Greanias shared with me the details of a personal religious experience he had at a Greek monastery where he, to paraphrase, visited the petrified hand of St. Mary Magdalene. Kneeling, he reached out to honor the artifact and found it to be warm to the touch and smoother than his own skin. This justification of his faith – that an ancient relic could possess the characteristics of a living person – is a challenging concept to grasp and accept for even the most open-minded. Adding to the complexity, send 30,000 believers to that same hand of St. Mary Magdalene and it's fair to assume that not a single person will return with the same sensations Greanias recalled so vividly – or any at all.

The beauty of faith and the power of believing, however, is that outside influences and opinions of what is and is not real simply do not matter. Faith is personal, and the experiences of believers are theirs and theirs alone. Therein lies a key difference between faith and sports: while both promote and celebrate a spirit of community among like-minded individuals, only in sports do we receive (require?) near-constant justification for our passion. When our belief – in a team, an athlete, a sport – wavers, we are always a triple play, diving catch or well-timed homerun away from a moment that restores and reinforces our proclamation of faith. The unbelievable play, described aptly, is actually a believable play. The action unfolds in front of us and in a packed ballpark with 30,000 pairs of eyes witnessing the same thing. And if we blink at the wrong moment, that little miracle called instant replay is always at the ready. The opportunity to confirm our faith in sports plays out in just about the most tangible way possible. This stands in stark contrast with believers forced to defend their devotion to the spectacularly unseen. So then, with that in mind, sports passion acts as the antithesis of religious belief.

"With the miraculous that comes from God, it's scary because we can't explain it," said Greanias. "At least in baseball, we see something we consider a miraculous catch or hit, or perhaps it's the timing of a homerun, like when the Red Sox beat the Tigers. At least you can explain that. It's more accessible to our understanding."

Greanias' casual reference to a Red Sox tilt against the Tigers as an example of the miraculous in sports required little explanation. I knew which game he was referring to as soon as those words tumbled out of his mouth. In the second game of the 2013 American League Championship Series, the down-and-out Boston Red Sox fell behind 5-0 late and faced a probable two-games-to-none deficit and the tough task of avoiding elimination on the road. As he had done during Boston's two previous successful World Series runs, slugger David Ortiz put the team on his back and with one mighty swing, sent a pitch soaring into the Red Sox bullpen beyond the outstretched glove of right fielder Torii Hunter to tie the game with a two-out grand slam. The Sox gave their jubilant congregation its own little miracle and evened the series at a game apiece. Weeks later, the team and its fans celebrated its third World title since 2004. Keep in mind that this Red Sox team aimed to embody the "Boston Strong" mantra all season long, borne as an expression of solidarity and support for a grieving city in the wake of the April 2013 Boston Marathon bombing. If that isn't a storybook ending, I don't know what is.

The game-tying homerun by David Ortiz was not a miracle. God did not will the ball beyond Fenway's short right field porch. Bostonians may disagree, but God is not a Red Sox fan. However, historians will undoubtedly remember this iconic moment as a gift from the Baseball Gods to a likable, close-knit band of bearded warriors and a beleaguered city recovering from tragedy. "Sports reflect life. We're all trying to get ahead we're all trying to do the best we can whatever that may be. [At sporting events] we're seeing someone be the best they can be, and it gives us hope that we can be that good in our pursuits," said Greanias. "We like to tune in to see somebody with a skill level above our own, and I don't know if people want to admit it or not, part of the admiration for anybody – whether it's an actor or an athlete – is they're using their God-given innate talents for good so you've got to respect and admire that. But as a sports fan, I don't have to put my belief system on the line, whereas with religion you're putting your belief system on the line. You're sticking your neck out."

3
PSYCHOLOGY AND SPORTS FANS

If we've established nothing else to this point, we can at least say with confidence that diehard sports fans endure a litany of emotions – for better or worse. The highest highs and the lowest lows, all wrapped around a six-month season, seven-game series, three-hour game or a single in-game course-correction that changes everything. For every instance of pure joy, as Father Greanias described it, there is an equal and opposite reaction happening simultaneously within the same ballpark by fans of the losing team. We all carry our own sense of hopeful optimism and excitement into each game, with perhaps a subconscious understanding that we're also putting our own mental health at risk. We do that knowingly, because we know that if the chips fall our way, the payoff is worth it.

Even still, while we try to block out any doubt that our favorite team can "win the big game," our psyche acts as a natural defense mechanism to prepare us for the devastation of defeat. Funny, preparing for disaster never really lessens the impact when the worst-case scenario occurs. While Coco Crisp's walk-off winner in game four of the 2012 American League Divisional Series sent the entire city of Oakland into an indescribable elation, Justin Verlander's mastery of that same team the next night to put a premature end to the Athletics' postseason dream left its fan base dumbfounded and demoralized. The earlier moment – the euphoria – doesn't soften the blow of the loss that followed, even if it felt inevitable from the first pitch. And no, telling yourself ahead of time that a stud pitcher with a history of shutting your team down will probably do so again definitely does not make you feel better when the inevitable becomes reality. It hurts, and it hurts for a good, long time. These experiences, the good and the bad, bring us closer to our team and our peers celebrating or commiserating alongside us in those hard plastic seats. They can serve as a catalyst for the evolution from casual fan to diehard. That road, however, is paved with emotional trauma. Why do we put ourselves through such torture?

Dr. Samuel Sommers, a psychology professor at Tufts University, believes sports fanaticism is one way people satisfy a basic human need. "People have a need for affiliation," he explained. "We're social animals and we feel a need to be with other people, to be members of groups, and to affiliate with others around us. It's part of normal psychological functioning.

"Think of it as the old psychology study where they put a rat in a cage and if he pushes a lever a certain number of times a pellet will come out. There is some partial reinforcement there, but it doesn't happen every time. You don't know when it's going to happen," Sommers said. "Granted, in the postseason or in a game seven, you know something amazing is going to happen one way or another – high risk, high reward, right? I think there is something to that in sports, this idea that something tremendous could happen and you could be a part of it."

To buy into the theory that fans either present for a sporting event or watching from home can be part of something "tremendous," as Sommers put it, you have to believe first and foremost that sports are important. Sommers believes fandom serves a basic human need of belonging to a group, so with that in mind, it is at least plausible to imagine that individual fans derive great personal significance from the sports world. Take into further consideration the economic impact of the multi-billion dollar sports industry that employs hundreds of thousands of workers, serves as a driver of civic pride and, on occasion, can accelerate the revitalization of downtrodden neighborhoods, and the argument becomes even stronger. Look no further than San Francisco, where the construction of Pacific Bell Park in 2000, led to a sweeping renaissance of the forlorn South Beach micro-neighborhood within the South of Market (SoMa) district. Once a decrepit wasteland, South Beach is teeming with action today thanks to posh housing developments and dozens of bars and restaurants that function almost as well during the offseason as on game day.

"Anything that has the ability to give somebody a sense of happiness, a sense of well-being, a sense of direction, a purpose in life and connections to others can be considered important," Dr. Wann explained, drawing on his research at Murray State University while discussing the societal importance of sports. "There are other pop culture activities that do that, but I would make the argument that sports is particularly well-situated to help achieve those personal and societal imperatives because it is a social activity. In sport, we often consume at the group level so you have the ability to bring people who wouldn't otherwise come together, together."

It is fair to assume that diehard sports fans align with Wann and believe all of the above. The games matter, the energy they pour into their chosen team is not wasted, and sports, with all of its joy and heartbreak, qualify as a worthy pursuit. To the fan, sports represent a hobby to be tended to and nurtured. Think of the diligent gardener hunched over for hours at a time primping and meticulously tweaking his or her blossoming creation. To stay connected to one's sports community, one must stoke the fire and remain plugged in. Primping, tweaking. Some people can separate real life – family, career, the everyday responsibility that comes with being an adult – from the world of sports. They come to the game and cheer, sing lustfully during the seventh inning stretch and then head home believing, win or lose, that a day at the yard is time well spent. These fans still react to the drama of sports as the action unfolds, but they check emotional baggage at the door on the way out. As fans, we are not suiting up and taking the field. We do not have million-dollar contracts to play the Children's Game and, generally speaking, our careers don't play out on-stage in front of thousands of onlookers. We are the onlookers. For some, however, the lines blur. The all-important sense of self and even self-worth tangles into the broader narrative surrounding their team. "They" and "their" become "we" and "our." The die-hard fan feels more involved and feelings associated with the team's success or failure become more pronounced. Emotional highs are higher, the lows are lower and the outcome on the playing field seeps into everyday life far beyond the boundaries of cement and steel. Experts stop short of citing predictive traits or calling out groups that could be more likely to allow sports to take up significant brain space. The concept of sports as escapism, however, might help us understand why a cross-section of diehards dives headfirst into the sporting life while others maintain perspective.

"The world is a threatening place. Psychologists have identified many strategies people use to help us cope with that threat, uncertainty and ambiguity, and it's something that you see play out in the world of being a sports fan," Sommers said. "When things aren't going great at work or your own workout regimen isn't living up to standards or relationships are on the rocks or whatever it is, there's still that allure of turning on the TV and watching that team that you identify with win the big game. We link our own ego and our self-esteem with sports teams, and it's an opportunity to, in some respects, feel good about ourselves even if things aren't going as well as we want them to.

"There are a lot of basic psychological needs and motivations that we have and there are a lot of different ways to fulfill them. We're able to fulfill them vicariously by affiliating with sports teams, so at a basic level being a sports fan is one of many ways through which we fulfill some of our basic psychological motivations and needs, and it's something that we do as humans to feel better about ourselves."

There is a touch of irony to the fact that Sommers, a man who studies human behavior and the psychology of everyday life, cites the April 30, 1988, game hosted by the Cincinnati Reds as his earliest memory of live Major League Baseball. Baseball-Reference.com records that game as an innocuous 6-5 loss to the New York Mets at Riverfront Stadium that dropped the Redlegs to an even record after 22 games. Historians, however, recall a different scene – one marred by bad behavior and, in the days that followed, an unprecedented punishment for a manager participating, albeit with a touch more physicality, in the time-honored tradition of arguing an umpire's call.

Reds manager (and baseball's all-time hit leader, I feel compelled to add) Pete Rose, who would soon be banned for life for gambling infractions, earned himself a 30-day suspension that afternoon. According to a statement from the Commissioner's Office, Rose received his punishment for "forcefully and deliberately shoving" first base umpire Dave Pallone while arguing a call in the ninth inning that allowed the go-ahead run to score. The suspension, handed down by Commissioner A. Bartlett Giamatti, was the most severe penalty given to a team manager for an on-field confrontation. Whether he may have dealt Rose a lesser punishment had it not been for the rowdy actions exhibited by those among the more than 33,000 attendees who chose to voice their displeasure by showering garbage onto the field will remain a mystery forever. Similarly, whether the "inflammatory and completely irresponsible remarks" made by Reds' radio broadcasters Marty Brennaman and Joe Nuxhall had any bearing on the outburst and fanned the flames of outrage is anyone's guess. Giamatti suffered a massive heart attack and died suddenly the following season, and more than 25 years have passed since the Commissioner's Office levied the heavy-handed blow. No manager has received such a lengthy punishment since.

Reflecting on that moment does make you wonder what drives people toward ugly reactions when confronted with sub-optimal situations presented by sports games. Baseball, perhaps more so than any professional sport, carries with it a distinctly human element that leads to a higher occurrence of human error than one might find in other sports. While that is certainly changing with increased reliance on instant replay, the fact remains that the probability that mistakes and blown calls will seep into a ballgame continues to be higher in baseball than any other sport. You might expect that fans might be more accepting when these errors occur. After all, "that's baseball." Yet, we are beside ourselves when an umpire misses a play or when a lucky bounce sends momentum into the opposing dugout. At our worst, we launch objects onto the field, we fight in the crowd; we are animals and it's ugly. Maybe it's just human nature. "There's always someone to hate," Sommers said. "I'm not going to blame sports for it, I think on some level it's a reflection of where we are as a human race."

He grew up in Ohio, but the adult Samuel Sommers is a diehard fan of the New York Yankees. This has proven to be a bit problematic since he relocated to the heart of Red Sox Nation. "We moved to Boston in 2003, which was a fine year to be a Yankees fan because the Yankees beat the Red Sox in Game Seven [of the American League Championship Series] and Aaron Boone hit that homer." No further description required. Boone's home run, a walk-off piece in the series' final game, sent the Yankees to the World Series and their hated rivals to the golf course. On any list of memorable playoff home runs, Boone's monumental blast into the Bronx night always bubbles to the top.

"I remember thinking, 'It's a good thing they won that game because I don't think I could live in this city if it had not gone well.' Little did I know that the next year, in 2004, the Yankees would go up three games to none, and they would, in the biggest choke job in the history of the playoffs, blow four games in a row and the Red Sox would win the World Series. It was insufferable."

Shortly after the Yankees' postseason meltdown, Sommers found himself overly frustrated by the successes of his team's fiercest rivals. The Red Sox dispatched the Yankees in the worst possible way and in an instant, a dominant season ended. However, real life didn't kick right back into gear for the young psychology professor. He couldn't get over the shock of a loss he had experienced vicariously through his chosen team. While his new city celebrated all around him, Sommers was irritable and agitated. Throughout the city and on campus, Red Sox flags waved proudly while banners were unfurled from windows and across buildings. For goodness sakes, the confetti is still clinging to the damp Boston roads following the team's celebratory parade! When will it end?

"There was a point when that was happening when I was like, 'I've got to not take this thing so seriously. It's not healthy for me,'" Sommers said. "I was a new father at the time. There's a baby, and it's not healthy for me to not be able to sleep at night and to wake up dreading getting out of bed in the morning because of what happened. That's insane."

For a while, Sommers distanced himself from the Yankees and from the sport he had followed intently since childhood. This strategy worked and he was able to remain in the Boston area to continue to pursue his teaching career despite working and living beyond enemy lines. He ignored Red Sox pandemonium, and Boston became home. "I'm still a Yankee fan and I'm still a big baseball fan, but I have learned that I can't do it that way. It doesn't work; it's not a healthy way for me to go through life being that agitated over the bad things because frankly, there's a point where you get more agitated over the bad than you get happy about the good."

Many people have experienced a similar emotional letdown to what Sommers felt while watching his team fall to pieces during the 2004 American League Championship Series. As he had described earlier in our discussion, that's the risk you take as a diehard fan: high risk, high reward. The Red Sox' moment of glory – the wave of jubilation that carried the city of Boston to the Promised Land – brought with it pain, heartbreak, and shock on the opposing side. Aftershocks rattled Yankees fans within New York's Bronx borough, the entire city, and fans of the Bronx Bombers nationwide. Yet they kept coming back for more. In fact, more than 54,000 bitter Yankees fans filed through the turnstiles on Opening Day to welcome in the 2005 season. Adding intrigue, the team played host to the defending World Champions – a stroke of genius by the schedule makers, though more than a little bit cruel to the melancholy home crowd. This time, the Yankees would prevail. While it may have been a hollow victory given the events of the previous October, as long as there are games to be played, a win is always going to be better than a loss. In early April, a few quick wins can push the shortcomings of the previous season a bit further in the rear view mirror. Four years would pass before the Yankees would be crowned champions again, which I suppose is a blink of an eye to some beleaguered franchises already discussed in this book. Still, despite the risk of enduring further torment, fans continue to subject themselves to punishing body punches with the outside chance that, hey, "this is our year." Today, we land the knockout blow.

"The experience of sitting there at some of those moments as a fan ... Your heart is racing, your blood pressure is way up in a way that, I mean it's very real, right? It's a very real experience," Sommers said. "It's incredibly physiologically arousing, and then something great happens and you release endorphins, and everyone around you is celebrating; it is this pure elation that you don't [often] experience. Most of us don't get that in our daily jobs or even in our relationships. People talk about the birth of a child or their wedding, but we don't get that kind of sensation too often."

Sommers adds credence to the idea that caring about games is not a trivial pursuit by mentioning the sensations felt during a sporting event in the same breath as the birth of a child or the exchange of wedding vows. After all, marrying your true love and creating a life bring such an intense and healthful joy. Attaining a similar degree of positive energy, even by just observing the performance of strangers, would seem to provide some benefit and usefulness in the lives of fans. I've often viewed sports in the way that non-fans might feel about their favorite television shows. We live in a time when seemingly every cable network is churning out situational "reality" programming about every topic imaginable – and for that matter, some that are altogether unimaginable. As far as I see it, sporting events serve as our last bastion of true reality entertainment. You can have your Kardashians and Real Housewives. I'll take my Swingin' A's and the Fightin' Phils. Sporting events cover a broad spectrum of experiences, just as television shows don't always knock it out of the park: hum-drum matchups (two teams with nothing at stake), edge-of-your-seat drama (tightly contested, well-played games), the bird's eye view of the human struggle (the battle between high-performance athletes) and comedy (errors, fouls, and flags). There is even a touch of romance if we tune into the play-by-play crew and listen as they wax nostalgic about the beauty of the game unfolding before our eyes. No installment follows the same script. Lest we learn nothing from sports history – baseball in particular, where the clock in the ballpark does not count down to anything and innings can last forever – it's never quite over until it's over.

Some people choose to park themselves on the couch and tune into the latest misadventures of cookie-cutter reality stars who stumble their way onto the cover of every grocery aisle magazine through a combination of good fortune and dumb luck. You pay for the pleasure of following their comedy of errors in monthly installments directed to the cable company. For the sports fan, you pay for a different variety of reality programming.

"I think sports get a bad rap. What do other people who are, 'more grown up' than I talk about? So they go out and talk about wine or they talk about the stock market ... why is that better?" Sommers said. "I mean, I don't know that that's any better. I suppose I could be into opera or classical music and I suppose that would have higher prestige to it in many quarters. I think it's [sports is] something that brings a fair number of people together. Like anything else, there are plusses and minuses, but I would argue it gets a bad rap sometimes."

4
HEALTH IMPLICATIONS OF DIEHARD FANDOM

Heartbreak sucks. The death knell ringing on a fizzling romance. A pet succumbs as pets do. When a loved one passes on, that old feeling creeps in with even more intensity. In fact, love and death are two of the more common catalysts for the sensations typically associated with heartbreak. And I would wager that most people can identify a few similar ways to describe the feeling itself: an aching, a sense of despondency, numbness, or overwhelming sadness. In trying times, it washes over like a wave. There is no escape. You can see it coming like a freight train in the distance, and yet you are powerless to stop the collision. Some people who have endured such pain describe an actual physical discomfort – most often in their chest – that accompanies these traumatic life events. The heart feels, in these instances, as though it is literally breaking into pieces. I've endured my fair share of heartbreak. After all, you'll recall that I'm a lifelong fan of the Philadelphia Phillies.

If you're a sports fan and the description of heartbreak sounds familiar, that's because it lurks around every corner in the sporting arena. We cannot escape the reminder that every game brings both the potential for positive and rewarding outcomes, and the possibility of complete and abject failure. The sports narrative is laden with heartbreak – it's almost obnoxious, actually. Watch any retrospective TV production about monumental sports moments and between the excitement and the magic, it's impossible to miss fans of the defeated standing together in shock. You can almost feel the sadness emanating from the screen as children bawl right along with the athletes, while grown men and women stare blankly into the distance. For every winner, there is a loser. For every thrilling victory, there is a devastating loss. And for every fan base exploding into a collective euphoria of unencumbered delirium, fans of the losing team deal with losing in a very real way. Blasted by the unstoppable freight train of suffering. Could it be that their hearts are breaking? In the moment, it certainly seems possible that a team loss could spark similar reactions to losses in other parts of our lives. I spoke with Meghan Laslocky, author of *The Little Book of Heartbreak: Love Gone Wrong Through the Ages*, to hear about the conclusions she had drawn after months of studying heartbreak as it exists at present and all the way back through ancient times. She described the literal pain associated with love gone awry, that sensation that bubbles up from the pit of your stomach or sticks in your chest like a dagger. As described, the feeling is a familiar one and I must admit that I have felt it while inside the ballpark. Where does it come from?

"Nobody knows for sure," she said. Darn. "There's no way to get a bunch of people in the room who are in the throes of heartbreak and actually having that feeling at that moment. Some people think it's that your rest and digest and your fight and flight impulses are being triggered at the same time. So it's kind of like two conflicting hormones being fired at the same time [causing] the responses to fight back or run away. Then at the same time you're digesting what has happened."

It is a surreal experience. This is particularly true if you happen to enjoy the distinct privilege of watching your team self-destruct on their home field. Surreal hardly does the moment justice, in fact, when it comes to do-or-die playoff games. The gaggle of dumbfounded fans stands together in total, deafening silence while their team slinks off the field amid a raucous celebration by the visitors. Sure, the victors might tamp down their celebration out of respect for the home team and the crushed onlookers. After all, they're not monsters. Even still, and particularly regarding the final moments of a Major League Baseball playoff run, which follows an absolute grind of a long – *long* – season, it is small consolation. The sadness is real and man, it stays with you.

I have been there on more than one occasion. During the fifth and final game of the 2013 American League Divisional Series in Oakland, the Athletics pinned their hopes on the right arm of rookie phenom Sonny Gray. Once again, Oakland had drawn the powerful Detroit Tigers, and I was in the crowd hoping for a repeat performance of the magic I had experienced the year prior. You may recall that my earlier playoff experience in Oakland concluded in glorious celebration after the Athletics had stolen victory from the jaws of defeat, as the saying goes. A year later, the experience fell on the opposite end of the spectrum and it was difficult to stomach. The Athletics have long drawn the ire of diehard fans for insisting on tarping the upper deck seats at decrepit O.co Coliseum. For these playoff games, the tarps stretching from foul pole to foul pole along the third tier of the stadium came off. The principal benefit of this disrobing – squeezing more fans into the ballpark – held immeasurable potential to transform the old yard into the loudest, most disruptive and intimidating confines for visiting teams. During the team's previous playoff run, Tigers' pitcher Justin

Verlander famously called the Coliseum crowd the most hostile environment he had ever pitched in, thanks to the intensity and volume of support for the home team. Now, one year later, ownership had committed to squeezing another 12,000 bodies into that cement oval. Aided by this newfound vocal strength, we were all beaming with excitement for the role we might play in throwing off the opposing squad with the power of our mighty roar. Unfortunately, we will never know just how loud that crowd could get as there was, from beginning to end, nothing to cheer about on this day. A weak ground out to second base, a lazy fly ball to left field ... Verlander (it's always Verlander, isn't it?) carved up the Athletics lineup with surgical precision for the second year in a row. He won while carrying a no-hitter – a no-hitter, for crying out loud – into the seventh inning. We stood and watched. We did our very best to will our team to, I don't know, maybe give us something akin to what we had felt the previous year. Instead, they were done. The magic was gone, the tank was empty, and the season ended with a feeble whimper.

As the Tigers celebrated around their ace after that final pitch, I felt numb. My brain was trying to come to grips with the fact that I wouldn't get to watch this team play, or enter this ballpark that I had made my second home, for nearly six months. Even amid the heavy sadness that covered the stadium like a blanket, I wanted to stay and soak in any last bit of baseball I could before the long winter slumber. The previous year, a friend and I did just that – wandered the concourse long after the final pitch until nearly every last soul had left the building. That was a moment of celebration and we did not want to let go. This was an instance of nostalgia and I just wanted to hang on a little bit longer. My friend had other plans.

"Let's get out of here. I can't be here anymore," he said to me. There would be no convincing him otherwise – he was halfway to the concourse before I could respond.

Closing the book on the 2013 season proved challenging for the two of us. We are both parents of young daughters and had shared so many beautiful moments at the ballpark together with our children. Personally, I'll never forget the day the Athletics clinched their second consecutive AL West title – a moment I shared with my daughter as we clapped, cheered, and danced with an enthusiastic home crowd. In this high-stakes world of sports fandom, that was about as high as you can get. A couple short weeks after watching the Athletics fail to make it out of the first round of the playoffs again, I was scraping the bottom of the emotional barrel. I resorted to thumbing longingly through the many photos I had taken of my little girl at the ballpark throughout the season. These captured memories served as a coping mechanism as I readied myself for a long winter without baseball, and without the happy conclusion we had all hoped for in Oakland. Such a bitter taste, this feeling of defeat.

As disappointment lingered for far too long, I began to wonder about the health implications of such a deep, emotional investment in the successes and failures of a sports team. Might I, a physically active male in good overall health, be doing irreparable damage to my body or mind by caring so deeply for the Oakland Athletics? Much to my relief, no. However, according to Dr. Bryan Schwartz, completing a cardiology fellowship at the University of New Mexico, it is not outside of the realm of possibility that some fans may suffer negative health outcomes because of their sports obsession.

"There are certain necessary components for there to be an association [between fandom and health-related incidents]," he explained. "Those necessary components are, first, being a diehard fan. The game has to be important, like a Super Bowl. The game has to be close and exciting. And when all of those prerequisites exist, at least a dozen studies have shown an association between a loss and things like increased heart attacks, increased heart-related deaths, increased sudden cardiac deaths and increased ER visits for arrhythmia."

In 2013, Schwartz collaborated with his peers Dr. Robert Kloner and Dr. Scott MacDonald to publish a study in *Clinical Research in Cardiology* titled, "Super Bowl outcome's association with cardiovascular death." In doing so, the researchers connected high-profile sporting events to negative impacts on a person's health following defeat in a hotly contested game. Their research took a hard look at the city of Pittsburgh, where in 2009, the Steelers pulled off a surprising Super Bowl victory after knocking out the Arizona Cardinals in dramatic fashion. Their studies found lower than usual instances of adverse health occurrences in Pittsburgh, home of the newly crowned champions. In an earlier study of Los Angeles, following a Super Bowl defeat of the Los Angeles Rams, Kloner had found that the opposite scenario had unfolded. His study cited higher than usual incidents, primarily in fans with existing health conditions – known or otherwise. According to Schwartz, traditional thinking surrounding negative health impacts and sporting events tied closely to the "fight or flight" response of the body, cited briefly by Laslocky as a possible reason why we *feel* heartbreak, due to the adrenaline surge caused by moments of excitement in the action. It makes sense: when the body is excited, blood pressure and heart rates rise. For people already susceptible or at risk of heart ailments, this can prompt an arrhythmia and cause an adverse outcome – namely, heart attack or even death. While that is a plausible explanation, any diehard sports fan who has lived through the emotional rollercoaster of fanaticism knows the logic, in a vacuum, is flawed. Assuming that our body endures the fight or flight response to some degree at just about any and every sporting event we attend – surely even the most mundane game features a moment or two of excitement sprinkled amid the snooze fest – why aren't more fans meeting their maker when the action-induced adrenaline surge reaches its climax? Schwartz could point to his own fight or flight moment to know there must be another connection between sports and heart trauma.

Schwartz, a Pittsburgh native, is himself a diehard Steelers fan. "Growing up in Pittsburgh, it's what you do," he explained. The Steelers famously had their own fight or flight moment and it happened on arguably the grandest stage of them all: Super Bowl 43 in 2009 against the Arizona Cardinals. In front of a live audience of more than 70,000 fans and another 151 million watching at home, the Pittsburgh Steelers stole the win with only 35 seconds remaining on the clock. What's more, eventual Super Bowl MVP Santonio Holmes sealed the victory with a heart-stopping toe-drag to pull in the winning touchdown in the corner of the end zone, sending the entire state of Arizona reeling. As Schwartz would describe it to me later, the first 59-and-a-half minutes of the game was an emotional roller coaster. Exceptional plays, back-and-forth lead changes, reversal calls on touchdowns late in the game and, of course, the final score with under a minute to play. Given that fans of both teams spent the entire game on the edges of their seats and glued to their TVs, the fight or flight response hypothesis would contend that diehards of both teams would have suffered increases in heart attacks. The intense emotional highs and lows of an up and down game do not favor one fan base over another. Instead, Schwartz and his peers found the opposite to be true. The city of Pittsburgh saw no increase in negative health events following the game. In fact, they found that in Pittsburgh after the Steelers won the Super Bowl, there were fewer heart-related deaths during the subsequent eight days.

"We hypothesized that perhaps the outcome of whether or not Santonio Holmes caught that ball or dropped that ball, whether or not the Steelers won or lost, affected Pittsburghers' mood," he concluded. "And had he dropped it, they would have been sad and depressed for a couple days. But he caught it, so they celebrated.

"It's known that mental health is associated with heart health. Having depression is associated with worse heart outcomes; having anxious symptoms is associated with more heart attacks. So perhaps, and we don't know this for sure, but we hypothesized that perhaps that's what we were observing."

So is it that simple? When your team loses, you get sad, and when you get sad, you die? Not so fast. Schwartz was quick to point out that, "If you don't already have heart disease, being sad is not going to give you a heart attack." What is telling, however, is that if you do have heart disease or other ailments that increase the likelihood that you may develop heart disease, sadness and depression can very much lead to heart attack. That said, the average fan isn't necessarily toeing the line each day.

Kloner's original study, "Comparison of total and cardiovascular death rates in the same city during a losing versus winning Super Bowl championship," appeared in the *American Journal of Cardiology* in 2009. This report reviewed the fallout from the Pittsburgh Steelers' victory over the Los Angeles Rams in the hotly contested 1980 Super Bowl. That game featured seven lead changes deep into the fourth quarter ultimately leading to a Steelers win in the up-for-grabs final minutes of action. In contrast with his later research with Schwartz, Kloner turned his attention to the city of Los Angeles as noted earlier in this chapter – home of heartbroken fans witnessing their Rams come up short in the Big Game. His findings are startling. In the two weeks following the Super Bowl defeat, incidents of all cardiac deaths in Los Angeles increased by 15 percent – spiking to 27 percent among women. In contrast, when the city's Raiders franchise breezed to victory in the 1984 Super Bowl, incidents of heart-related deaths declined. Kloner's conclusions suggest that the emotional distress and the lingering psychological impact associated with intense games could lead to higher death rates among men, women, and older adults in instances of negative game outcomes.

The risk of suffering fatal consequences due to the performance of sports teams is a small one for the average fan. Eat and sleep well, exercise and maintain a healthy lifestyle and, in most cases, you can ride the wave of the sports-induced adrenaline surge with a relatively clear mind. The slightly more nuanced threat – the more prominent issue at hand – is the underlying trigger for many of the health outcomes Schwartz studied, good and bad: our emotional fragility as sports fans. Certainly, relying on outside influences for happiness and personal enrichment is not exclusive to sports fans. Many interests deliver excitement, satisfaction and, occasionally, disappointment. However, where sports fans differ is in enduring an extreme range of emotional fluctuations across a short time – be it a full season with its pleasing or disappointing conclusion right down to the rapid-fire momentum swings within a single game, inning, or play. We get moody. Some are bipolar. We are emotionally unstable. A funny lot indeed, my fellow sports fans.

Trying to pinpoint the impacts of this kind of outcome – how the sporting bubble affects our lives once we are back on the outside again – proves more difficult. Who's to say that my dip in performance at work can be attributed to the devastating playoff loss that I'm still grappling with beneath the surface? Or, on the other hand, is it simply because I am not getting enough sleep? Complicating matters further, what if I'm not sleeping well *because* I am still thinking about my team's abrupt playoff ouster, thus leading to poor performance at the office? Then again, maybe I am just a terrible employee. Other elements influencing our mental state muddy the equation. Suffice it to say, being a sports fan makes us happy and, at times, sad. Sadness affects us outside of the ballpark.

The basic human need for affiliation covered in an earlier chapter tells us a lot about sports fanaticism and the connectedness we feel with our team and its performance. We are social creatures and we long for community. We strive for a feeling of belonging and the mutual understanding that exists when people come together and enjoy shared interests. At the stadium, we look around the horde and nod knowingly to our fellow fans. *You're in on it too, huh?* This secret society gathers frequently, dresses the same, chants in the same way, and even sits and stands in unison. The rewards – emotional satisfaction and justification of our boundless commitment – are plentiful in good times. At other times, loyalty is tested. I have found that some within our tribe view the times when our teams have nothing left to play for as validation of their fan status. When things are going sideways, we wear our loyalty like a badge of honor: "I stuck with them when no one else did" and, therefore, "I am a real fan." No one wants to wear the scarlet letter of Bandwagon Fan – there is no greater insult than to imply that one might cut and run when the going gets tough. To avoid such a label, of course, means we must at times watch terrible, terrible games. We must endure the emotional self-flagellation of rooting haplessly for bad teams. Doing so, we tell ourselves, will make victory all the more delicious in the end.

Part of it is fear, and it ties back to the social element, the sense of community. Most fans, sticking with one team long enough, will endure more than a few games that are just painful to watch, plain and simple. How is it going to look if we get up and leave? Will I lose status with the friends I've made right here in these very seats? You can think of it as an investment: as fans, we invest in a team. The value of our investment fluctuates not only based on the outcome on the field, but rather, on the experiences at the ballpark with fans in our everyday lives. Baseball is the only major sport that features enough contests to afford teams the opportunity to lose 100 or more games. Perhaps the experience of the super-fan – waving his flag in the bleachers and treating every half-empty Tuesday night game as a meet up opportunity to share stories and commiserate with new friends – is better for it. Knowing we are supporting our team through every bad moment – and by proxy, our community – earns us credibility. Super-fan status grows stronger as the bandwagon fans fall off the cart and head for the exit with every bases-loaded walk and every horrible swing. Surviving the bad times helps fans identify even more closely with both the team on the field and their fellow diehards in the stands. We believe that suffering through one ugly loss after another propels us to the front of the line of the imagined VIP queue, where the glory of sweet victory awaits. And it will come. In time, it always does. In the meantime, diehard fans must work at maintaining perspective to keep the bad times from overwhelming their senses and, in the worst instances, overcoming their lives away from the game.

5
BASEBALL HELL

On their run to the 2010 World Series title, their first since moving to San Francisco in 1958, the Giants built a marketing machine around the concept of torture. Riding a wave of nail-biting, edge-of-your-seat one-run victories, walk-off magic and improbable comebacks, the Giants galvanized a movement among a rejuvenated and excitable fan base. The momentum started in April and ended with the city's first parade down Market Street in honor of its quirky baseball franchise.

Here was a ragtag collection of personalities and oddballs marching down the street with confetti raining down from the sky and thousands of fans following a caravan of slow-moving trolleys to City Hall. The players, on the outskirts of relevance for much of the season, came together for a frantic run of success in the season's final days. Overcoming nearly insurmountable odds, they took the NL West division during a season-ending series against the backsliding San Diego Padres. The city loved their team, which included shaggy-haired pipsqueak Tim Lincecum (who just happened to also be a two-time Cy Young Award winner), predicting hopefully that the team's fan base would have "beer flowing and smoke in the air" after the final chapter of the 2010 season had been written. Injury-prone washout Aubrey Huff handled first base duties and occasionally drifted into the outfield to play a subpar bordering-on-comical left field. He also carried the team at times and completely revitalized a sagging career. For better or worse, Huff made the rally thong "a thing" that people actually talked about and celebrated publicly. At third base, rotund Pablo Sandoval defied gravity and dodged questions about his ballooning body with the same unexplainable dexterity he used to snare balls down the line. He also seemed to hit just about anything thrown near the plate and could even scamper from bag to bag with sneaky speed. Simply put, this weird team just kept winning all the way to the end. All of this winning sparked a feel-good party atmosphere at every game played in picturesque – and packed – AT&T Park on San Francisco's glorious waterfront. During the 2010 season, there was no hotter party spot in San Francisco than AT&T Park. Yet, the refrain of, "It's torture!" resonated throughout the city streets.

That's not torture. Not even close.

Torture is life as a Miami Marlins fan.

The life cycle of a sports team follows a predictable trajectory. Draft well, groom prospects, build around homegrown talent, fill in the gaps with free agents and scrap heap pickups, and ride the wave to championship glory. Then, replace aging stars with the next generation of homegrown talent and watch the cycle repeat. The best teams can maintain consistency and, as they say in the business, keep the window of opportunity for multiple title runs open a bit longer than odds makers might predict. Of course, this is the best-case scenario. Not everyone follows the blueprint to a T, and even those that do wind up falling short more often than not. After all, it begins with building a deep minor league system chock full of marquee prospects. When you're pulling promising athletes out of high school and college at 18 or 19, and signing international free agents before they can drive, dumb luck plays a factor just as much as anything else when it comes to getting it right.

Some teams can cheat the system, as you might imagine, and bypass the first few stages entirely by jumping right into free agency with both feet and deep pockets. I probably don't need to explain to you that the teams best-suited to pursue this path reside in New York and Los Angeles. That said, a certain New York franchise did just so happen to send a pair of Hall of Fame-bound home-grown stars on a retirement tour in consecutive years – arguably the best closer in the game in Mariano Rivera and "Mr. November" Derek Jeter. Even the richest franchises rely on drafting well and plucking diamonds from the rough from time to time in the grand guessing game of amateur scouting.

There is a third path, however. A road littered with shattered dreams, damaged hearts, and broken spirits. The signposts are illegible and the trail is disorienting. You see, on this path, even progress is misleading. You take a few steps forward only to realize you are actually just going in circles. This is the journey of the tormented Miami Marlins fan.

The Miami Marlins, known originally as the Florida Marlins, put South Florida on the Major League map in 1993. Donning the loudest hue of teal to ever grace a base-ball diamond, the league's newest franchise road-tripped their way across the state in the months leading up to their inaugural season to drum up excitement, sell tickets and steal fans away from the perennial division champion Atlanta Braves – the closest professional franchise geographically. On the surface, the Marlins made too much sense. When you think about it, it is surprising that the state of Florida did not have a professional baseball team before the Marlins came along. Before each new season, half of the league makes its pilgrimage to the sandy beaches and blue skies of sunny Florida for Grapefruit League spring training action. Fans pile into tiny ballparks speckled throughout the state to catch a glimpse of their favorite stars and get the high-touch attention most only dream about at the massive big league caverns that stretch from coast to coast. That's in addition to the intense passion for the sport woven into the DNA of Florida's immigrant population and its sandlot kids at play from Tallahassee to the Keys. As apt here as anywhere else, this is baseball country. However, locals had little choice but to cast their lot with teams outside state lines until the Marlins joined the party.

Excitement for a professional franchise in Florida reached a fever pitch in 1993 and more than three million fans filed into the ballpark that first season. There was a strong showing at the gates despite watching their expansion team drop more than 90 games and finish far behind the surprise division-winning Philadelphia Phillies. The Phillies flipped the script in 1993, catapulting out of the basement and into the champagne-soaked dressing room that comes standard with a league title. Something similar would happen to the Marlins a few years down the road, but in reverse order. We will get to that in a moment.

Eclipsing the three million mark for attendance is no small feat. Still today, the Marlins first season goes down in history as its most successful as a box office draw. The Marlins finished 33 games behind the Phillies that year with a tally of 64-98. No one cared – the lowly New York Mets prevented the Marlins from finishing dead last. Great success. That attendance figure stands today as a club record by a huge margin: the second-highest total falls 700,000 patrons shy. Florida rocked teal-colored glasses during the team's first season, but that would all change. The Marlins fan base – new to the league, but not to the game – experienced its first dose of pain during the second year of the Florida Pro Baseball Experiment. Sadly, it was just the smallest taste of the misery to come.

Many baseball fans growing up in the 1980s and 1990s lost their youthful exuberance for America's national pastime on August 12, 1994. Following months of bickering between millionaire players and their billionaire owners, Major League Baseball executed its fourth work stoppage in the previous 22 years. This one, which lasted 232 dreadful days, had staying power. For many impressionable Marlins fans, the strike served as an early encounter with the dark reality of professional sports. The beautiful façade of pure athletic excellence contrasted sharply with the greed and the power-driven machine of a multi-billion dollar empire lurking in the shadows.

The years that followed set in motion the sweeping generalizations and perceptions of Marlins fans as we know them today: fickle, fair-weather, and perhaps worst of all, disloyal. After three million people turned in their ticket stubs in that inaugural year to watch mediocre baseball inside the uncomfortable confines of football-first Joe Robbie Stadium, the team would eclipse two million just one more time in their short history. That would come four years later when the Marlins took home the game's top prize as World Series Champions. In between, the entire league endured an epic hit to its popularity following the 1994 labor strike, which ripped out the hearts of fans everywhere and exposed Major League Baseball for what it is, at its core: a business. I remember the day business interfered with my favorite sport as if it was yesterday. This might sound weird to the casual fan, but to live through it and see the soap opera in real time as players and owners sniped at one another was to watch a little piece of the magic disappear. The game itself took a backseat that summer, and what came to the fore was just plain ugly: grown men threatening each other over contract terms, grandpas scolding spoiled 20-somethings and on the outside looking in, frustrated fans begging and pleading for everyone to figure it out and keep playing. Frankly, as an impressionable teenager who ate, slept, and breathed the game of baseball during the early-to-mid-1990s, I never wanted to hear the term "collective bargaining agreement" ever again after that summer.

In the seasons immediately following the strike the Marlins did their best to encourage fans to get back to the yard, but the damage was done. Fans stayed away in Miami, as they did everywhere else, for a long time. In any city, the best way to boost attendance and heal the wounds of betrayal is by winning. In 1997, that was exactly what the Marlins did. Improbable as it was, coming just four years after the feel-good story of Major League Baseball expansion into a region that had previously seen pro ball cease play each year in late March, the Florida Marlins won it all. Rooting for an expansion team typically demands patience and recognition that you're going to be rooting for a losing team for quite a while. Fans of the Seattle Mariners, for example, are still waiting for their lovable losers to capture the league's grandest prize after nearly 40 years and a few close – but not too close – calls. In 1997, the Marlins gave new hope to every fledgling club that with the right mix of talent, youth and coaching, anything could happen. That season offered proof that any team can rise from the ashes to shock the world and treat their fans to an October parade. For a winning team built with a healthy mix of homegrown talent, free agent finds, and late-season acquisitions like the longtime Phillies catcher Darren Daulton, all of the usual clichés apply. They had leadership, and they had chemistry. Daulton "brought the locker room together." Young players like Livan Hernandez and Edgar Renteria played with energy that showed how much they "just love playing baseball." They had it all, and by God, it seemed sustainable. Could they be entering an era of dynastic baseball in south Florida?

You know the story from there. The dynasty was not to be. In fact, ownership didn't even wait to sweep up the ticker tape before dismantling the league's feel-good story of 1997 and ushering in a period of distrust and paranoia among its most loyal and broken fans. Riding the high of Florida's first pro ball championship, the Marlins won 54 games the following year and really, the defending champs never had a chance – both on the field and at the ticket office. Attendance dropped by more than 650,000 year-over-year. In 1998, 1,750,000 fans filed into the stadium to have their hearts ripped out repeatedly. Ownership, led by Blockbuster head Wayne Huizenga, didn't even give the burgeoning fan base a chance to build on the championship momentum. In most cities, a title victory creates a grace period and a spirit of goodwill that brings fans back to the stadium in droves. For the Marlins, ownership brought baseball to Florida and then appeared to do its best to wipe it off the map.

I remember how people scoffed about the Marlins securing a beautiful new state-of-the-art ballpark in Miami a few years ago after several years of poor attendance at the old retrofitted multi-purpose they had called home since 1993. The team often cited the wet and humid weather as the grand excuse for why their fans preferred to consume Marlins baseball in air conditioning rather than choosing to melt away at the ballpark. In muggy south Florida, the constant threat of rain and heat necessitated the construction of a domed ballpark experience and that, they said, would bring the fans back to live baseball. What they failed to acknowledge at the time was the need for an apology: an apology to a fan base on life support due to the yo-yo team-building philosophy deployed by the team's front office. A few short years after the build-it-up and tear-it-down experience of 1997 and 1998, the Marlins ownership, refusing to get out of their own way, did it all again. In 2003, the team again secured a Wild Card playoff slot – the new reality of divisional playoff baseball born out of a desire expressed by the commissioner's office to bring Major League ball into the 21st century with a commonly accepted playoff format adopted by all other major leagues. Led again by a beautiful blend of old and new, the Marlins brought a second World Series title to south Florida that year. They did it on the backs of veterans like future Hall of Fame catcher Ivan Rodriguez, slugging third baseman Mike Lowell, and young flamethrower Josh Beckett, who at 23 years of age pitched the decisive game in the Bronx against the heavily favored New York Yankees. Joining Beckett in the Marlins' latest youth movement included 21-year-old sensation Dontrelle Willis and a baby-faced 20-year-old named Miguel Cabrera. Cabrera, of course, would go on to become the first Triple Crown winner (league leader in batting average, home runs, and runs batted in) the league had seen in more than 30 years. Famously, and in true Marlins fashion, he accomplished the feat in another team's uniform.

Unlike the punk job of 1998, the second fire sale started as a slow burn before the return of the more familiar explosion from a few years prior. At first, owner Jeffrey Loria kept the gang together. Much to everyone's surprise, he even added to it by signing powerful first baseman Carlos Delgado. This experiment with roster consistency survived two middling seasons before the new owner, like his predecessor, lit another match and ignited another dynamite blast following the 2005 campaign. No amount of winning can repair the collateral damage of enduring not one, but two roster mulligans in less than a decade. Marlins ownership had crossed the line. Then, seven years after their beloved ball club ripped their hearts out for the first time, fans responded. In truth, they responded by not responding. Despite outperforming expectations – in 2006, the season after the team had jettisoned nearly every tier-one ballplayer on the roster and carried the sport's lowest payroll – and hanging tough in the Wild Card hunt until a late-season fade, Marlins fans would not be fooled a second time. The team drew just north of one million in paid attendance, though actual gate figures were substantially lower. Several promising seasons following the first massive sell-off had attendance creeping back toward pre-fire sale figures, but the impact proved insignificant. Marlins baseball barely drew 14,000 per game in 2006 and for the rest of the decade the Marlins would not approach 20,000 again.

This fan base, as true in the mid-1990s as it is today, is a melting pot of Floridians who had waited a lifetime for baseball to come to Florida. A blend of old-timers that switched alliances from other big league clubs in order to support their home state and young people who had only known Marlins baseball were now bleeding out into the Gulf of Mexico. This delightful collection of disparate cultures, creeds and backgrounds had come together to throw their support behind a fledgling franchise, but were now dying inside. The diehard Marlins fan had been broken down and could no longer take the pain. Meanwhile, onlookers from every corner of the U.S. and the national media landscape began to toss barbs toward this dispirited lot. Somehow, Marlins fans – all three of them? – were unworthy of our sympathy. Marlins highlights on ESPN, few and far between as they were, became scarcer and amounted to startling images of home run balls bouncing around in rows and rows of empty seats. Where were the fans? Why does Florida even have a team? No one shows up to games. To this day, the narrative festering around the Marlins and their fans is inescapable. While the team itself – even more precisely, the front office – may not deserve compassion, must we dismiss an entire fan base so quickly? Is there not a connecting thread that binds diehards together? Is it impossible to imagine that jerking people around like a bunch of lapdogs would eventually take its toll?

"What people don't understand is that we went from an expansion franchise to winning the World Series in a 'new market,' but we weren't just a bunch of people who were not very complex individuals and didn't understand the game. We didn't all of a sudden chuck the idea and go back to staring at the sun on the beach. We actually know a lot about the game," said John Ricard, founder of the popular Marlins blog, MarlinsNation.com.

The frustration in Ricard's words is not just in your imagination or my own emphasis. Ricard, the foremost defender of the Marlins beleaguered franchise despite its endless shock and awe roster purges, spoke to me late one night in January about his experience loving a team that most people might find hard to love. I could feel the weight of his struggle as a fan rooting for a team often ridiculed for having the league's least-supportive fan base. It was shortly after New Year's Day – perhaps the quietest time of year for baseball, as the flurry of pre-holiday moves subside and most major league front offices take a much-needed breather. January also marks the time of year when fans start to go stir-crazy and, you know, spend two hours on the phone with other diehards they had never spoken to before. This was one of those nights.

Ricard pulled for the Atlanta Braves while growing up in Florida during the pre-Marlins era of the 1980s and early 1990s. In a state without a professional baseball franchise, all locals could do was grab hold of the closest franchise and dream of a team they could call their own. For Ricard, that reality came true when the Marlins brought teal back into style and had every kid across the state ready to forsake their existing allegiances for the new hometown nine. "I think that's kind of what solidified it for me was moving back to Miami, back to home where our family was from and where my roots were," Ricard said.

Enthusiasm for this new team ricocheted from every corner of the state during that inaugural season. Players met with fans, reporters profiled future stars, and palpable excitement for professional ball in the Sunshine State manifested from Jacksonville to Miami. As young fans do, a teenaged John Ricard closed his eyes and explored a fantastical world where the expansion Marlins would buck convention and best the predictions bandied about by national sports pundits. You see, fans have permission to do that. So as a fan, you're allowed to get excited that the Kansas City Royals left Jeff Conine unprotected in the expansion draft and that your Marlins had the wherewithal to snap him up. You can dream that an unknown import from the Japan Professional League named Orestes Destrade would become the next great slugger to return from an overseas tour with jaw-dropping power. History confirms that Destrade would not transform into a present-day Cecil Fielder, of course. Destrade hit 20 home runs that first season and knocked but five more before falling out of the league forever. But that didn't matter. Excitement was in the air and Florida was feeling good. Marlins Fever soared to an all-time high when Charlie Hough, the wily master of the knuckleball and native son of nearby Hialeah, Florida, tossed a first-pitch wobbler for a strike on Opening Day. Never mind that the pitch was two feet off the plate. Mark it down in the record books in ink: Florida finally had its own Major League team.

"This was Florida, where my roots were – back home so to speak. Growing up in south Florida, baseball is a big thing – baseball is year-round down there," Ricard explained. He went to the trouble of justifying the idea of Florida baseball, but I was completely on-board from the moment we realized together that Florida had been without a pro team for 100 years. "It's almost a no-brainer. Why wouldn't Florida have a Major League Baseball franchise? [Florida hosts] Spring Training every year, and Miami alone is just a collection of people who enjoy baseball from the Caribbean. Puerto Ricans, Cubans, Colombians, Dominicans, and Venezuelans – a natural fit."

You have to remember that Ricard, arguably the staunchest defender of Marlins baseball, switched allegiances as a teenager. All the principal elements addressed in this book pertaining to what draws fans to sports teams apply to Ricard's situation. Proximity: his rooting interests no longer rested on the wrong side of state lines. Sense of community: as a Floridian rooting for a Florida team, Ricard had a readymade network of like-minded people all around him. And importantly, the feeling of ownership: this was pro ball in Miami. The Major Leagues had come home.

The story might have played out differently had Ricard not moved back to his childhood home in Miami from Jacksonville – known as a border town featuring a confounding mix of rooting allegiances. The forces of Mother Nature brought Ricard home just as the Marlins were planning their own move into pro ball. Beyond sports teams, the other connecting thread that binds every coastal-living Floridian together is the fear, lying in wait until the late summer months, that seeps into their hearts and minds as hurricane season approaches. Hurricane Andrew hit in August 1992, pounding the coastline and forcing many families to pick up the pieces and start again. Ricard answered the rallying cry to stand side-by-side with his father to rebuild houses throughout the Miami area and help people get back on their feet. What started as a short-term project to support family members in distress turned into a much more involved experience that required a move back to Miami just as the Marlins were opening for business. Suddenly, cheering for a sports team representing a distant city, with an entirely different set of cultural touch points, traditions and life circumstances seemed less relevant. The ties that tethered Ricard to the Atlanta Braves began to fray as he started to establish a personal connection with a fresh, new ball club more closely aligned with his culture, his community, and his Miami lifestyle.

Much like its unpredictable fall weather, the life of a Marlins fan is anything but stable. The highs of expansion and World Series titles juxtaposed against the lows of the fire sales that hit this franchise like clockwork following any especially satisfying run. It's enough to spark a clinical diagnosis of paranoia and schizophrenia in anyone. Few can argue that ownership didn't play a leading role in damaging Marlins fans before they even had a chance to amass an army. In keeping with the theme of paranoia, you can build an argument that the real game played out behind closed doors: a group of spoiled executives toying with the fragile psyche of its battered fan base for sport. *We're not driving the fans away fast enough – let's make a move!* To this point, we have not even mentioned the Marlins third owner, John Henry, who took over the reins for a short stretch between Huizenga and Loria and restored a sense of hope in the city's beaten-down fans. The goodwill did not last long. Perhaps frustrated by the lack of progress toward a new home for his new franchise, Henry cried poor and left the team for greener pastures after three short years. His exodus led him to one of the league's richest and most storied franchises, the Boston Red Sox. Irony is not lost on the perceptive Marlins fan.

"As a Marlins fan, it's like your dad left for a hotter wife or something," Ricard told me. "What the hell, he can purchase the Red Sox, but couldn't purchase a new stadium in south Florida? You're left scratching your head, and then Loria comes in who owned the Expos and there's nothing but bad news about this guy – look what he did in Montreal."

Loria, in concert with Major League Baseball Commissioner Allen "Bud" Selig, sold his Montreal Expos to a consortium comprised of the other 29 Major League ball clubs. Before long, the team moved out of Canada altogether and Washington, D.C. had its first pro baseball team since the Senators made camp in Arlington, Texas to become the Rangers in 1972. Amid the cloud of confusion, negotiations, and legal issues – Loria and Major League Baseball battled a Racketeer Influenced and Corrupt Organizations Act (RICO) lawsuit in the exchange of ownership – Henry pawned the Marlins off on Loria for more than $158 million and the city of Miami braced itself for trouble.

In a refreshing twist and in direct contrast with the negativity percolating throughout the rest of the Marlins fan base, Ricard remained optimistic as the Loria era began in earnest. His optimism could be due, in part, to the fact that he had fled Miami for graduate school at Florida State University in faraway Tallahassee. They say that absence makes the heart grow fonder. Separated from the action, Ricard turned to the Internet and began to grow nostalgic for his flawed team and its clown car front office. In those days, forums were a relatively new outlet for sports fans to stay connected to their teams and one another. In doing so, Ricard found himself in the odd position of serving as Loria's chief (only?) defender in various online forums and chat rooms. Arguing and debating the prospects for Jeffrey Loria's Marlins takeover, Ricard discovered the sense of community he had lost amid his relocation. Some people he came across shared poorly constructed arguments, and others presented points and counter-points that he struggled to debunk. Across the board, however, what Ricard found in his interactions were Marlins fans, pure and simple. People who shared his passion for teal and who had suffered the same emotional trauma this beloved team had inflicted on him through the years. Marlins Nation had arrived – and now it just needed a place to call home.

"I built the site [MarlinsNation.com] with the idea in mind that it was a way for Marlins fans to get exposure for being knowledgeable baseball people, and for being good fans," he said. "I always felt that I needed to stand up and defend us Marlins fans in some public way. That's the reason why I took the name 'Marlins Nation' – to serve as a beacon of Marlins fandom. There are good Marlins fans out there and we do know something about the game."

All of this, amid a tumultuous ownership change that brought threats to what little comforts the young fan base had enjoyed. Here was a young man simultaneously advancing his own education at FSU, while serving to educate and engage others in his support of a team that had let him and every other fan down on, at the very least, two distinct occasions. Nevertheless, in this irrevocably broken romance, at least Florida had its team. In a 100-year-old league, Florida had a legitimate professional squad even if its various owners weren't quite sure how to run the operation without alienating every single person who had walked through the turnstiles. No one could take that away. Or could they?

"All the sudden, you have the evil 'C' word coming around – contraction," Ricard whispered the word and I almost felt like hanging up the phone and taking a shower. As he said, contraction is evil. Imagine for a moment that an ownership group deemed you and your fellow fans no longer worthy of a pro team – and in this case, after a laughably short time in the market. That's a tough pill to swallow, and the pain is real. "For me in particular as a Marlins fan, I've come all this way and I've climbed on board. You guys [the team] got me with the free candy at the beginning, but now here I am years later and I am still a fan. It [affected] me psychologically or maybe emotionally. It's my hometown; it's where I grew up. Otherwise, what fan would go through all this crap? You wouldn't go through this in a relationship, let alone a team."

That's the kicker. You certainly would not hope to go through any of this – deception, dishonesty, lack of regard for feelings, and so much more – in a relationship. Yet, we do endure it as fans. We allow ourselves to be jerked around based on the whims of an extremely orchestrated and lucrative business. But when things are good, boy are they good. In a short period, the Marlins diehard has experienced the apex that the sport of baseball can deliver. It's because of that glimpse of what might be possible if the team ever got their act together again, coupled with a sense of community felt while celebrating other small successes, that fans continue to endure the lowest of lows. Marlins lows are atypical of the traditional fan experience. While it is true that every team has suffered a fair share of heartache, finding a collection of fans that have experienced the level of abuse driven by the Marlins front office is an exercise in futility. When you're scoffing at Marlins fans, dubbed the worst in baseball by folks who write about that sort of thing, consider that the good times in Miami are countered by the most heart-wrenching destruction and psychological damage imaginable within the realm of sport. Those who stick with the team suffer an inordinate amount of pain, and it's worth asking yourself if you would put up with it too.

So with that in mind – with the vicissitudes, roster purges, false hopes, shifty ownership groups, threats of contraction, you name it – why do Marlins fans continue to put up with the torture?

"There's a love-hate relationship, and love and hate seem to spring from the same well," Ricard explained. "Being a fan is not simply being an observer – you're not just objectively observing something. You have some skin in the game and you identify with the team maybe because of the city you're from – it's a part of your life. There's always a part of the self [that is] involved and I think that's what makes a transition from simply being an observer of action [by other] human beings out there to being a fan."

The point Ricard made about having skin in the game is an interesting concept to consider. Technically speaking, we do not have any skin in the game. We don't make any money based on the outcome of the on-field competition, and we don't have any stake in the players on the field. Most fans do not have any familial connections or friendships with professional ballplayers. They play a game and we watch. But we don't just watch, do we? There's something deeper involved, and I don't think Ricard is too far off the mark when he raises a difference between observing and being a fan. As a fan, we are pulling for a preferred out-come. We want our team to win. We also want to high-five strangers sitting around us, and we want to incite a stadi-um-wide chant of "Let's go [insert team name here]." Why do we wish to do these things? The more fans I spoke with while writing the book you hold in your hands, the more I kept coming back to one thing: community. Camaraderie. In the same way that excitement may spike slightly when you come across someone at a party that might have seen and enjoyed the same movie you just saw, sports fandom brings people together in celebration of a common interest and we're all pulling on the rope in unison. A small town of 40,000 people crammed into rows of seats and crowded concourses – all cheering, all with skin in the game.

And that brings us back to the plight of the Marlins fan. As with any professional franchise, the Marlins have bandwagon fans. They have bad fans and fans that don't understand the game. Just like any team, the Marlins have fans that might reach out and grab a ball that is in-play simply because they just don't "get it." All of that now out in the open, the Marlins also have great fans. In the state of Florida, particularly in south Florida, a thriving immigrant population has grown up with the game from sandlot to sandlot. This is a community with a rich baseball tradition, even if its foray into pro ball is relatively new. Marlins fans bear the wounds of a beaten and battered bunch, but even still, the diehards like John Ricard keep coming back for more.

"I'd want to clarify with other fans that there are Marlins fans out there and we've endured our share of pain and we continue to back our team. For that, I think we all stand and share that common bond," Ricard told me. "We endure the pain for the very reason we would in any relationship if it means something to us. We put ourselves into it and that's what I've been trying to express as a Marlins fan for a while. We're not just fickle, south Florida beachgoers that show up when they win and say 'ah, this is boring, we're leaving.' It's not that simple. We don't show up because we're so angry about what we had with the team before that was blown up."

As an Oakland Athletics fan, this whole conversation hit a little close to home for me. Many of the themes Ricard touched on – threats of contraction and relocation, stadium drama, owners with low approval ratings, and more – made me wonder if the perceptions of Oakland Athletics fans mirror those of Ricard's Miami Marlins, and if so, what might cause common threads to emerge clear across the country. The broad perception of Marlins fans is that they don't exist. As Ricard so vehemently contended, that is simply not true. Athletics fans are not without their critics even if they don't suffer quite the same negative perceptions as Marlins fans. Of course, the criticisms are there. The Athletics seldom sell out their games, and followers of other teams have been known to scoff at A's fans while they're busy laughing at the idea of Marlins diehards, especially when compared to the rejuvenated San Francisco Giants fan base. For all the recent success and renewed local excitement for the Bay Area's "other" team, the Athletics remain in the bottom half of the league when it comes to attendance. No one doubts that the fans that do show up are among the best in the league. Even still, it's surprising that such a lovable, fun-to-watch ball club – combined with its recent stretch of winning baseball – would prove to be such a terrible draw day-in and day-out. Once you start to look beyond the numbers and dig into broader context of the fan experience, the connecting threads between the Marlins and A's emerge. Simply put, everyone hates Lew Wolff.

Wolff is part of the Athletics ownership group, and for all of his team's on-field success, he has not ingratiated himself with local fans. To be fair, it is highly probable that Wolff wants the Athletics to succeed in Oakland. After all, owners typically see success on the balance sheets when teams succeed on the field. I imagine that Wolff, contrary to the belief of many of the team's most ardent supporters, is a fan himself and he wants other fans to both enjoy the product that the front office assembles each year and experience a similar level of enjoyment at the ballpark. It is also worth acknowledging that while Wolff may be both the vocal and visible leader of the ownership group, he is only the team's minority owner. John Fisher, the man who holds the purse strings, is its silent majority owner and is likely the man calling most of the shots. Yes, Wolff does endure an extraordinarily weighty amount of criticism from fans who refuse to believe he cares about the team, its host city, and them. The level of Wolff's love of the Oakland Athletics is not widely known by its fans, of course, because the owner-fan relationship is typically not a direct one. In other words, an owner would need to become heavily involved in the daily dealings of the franchise a la George Steinbrenner to own real estate within the forefront of fan consciousness. The other way to establish a direct relationship with fans is to buy their favorite team and then immediately give them every reason to dislike you. Shortly after purchasing the ball club, Wolff and Fisher determined that the team needed a new ballpark (he was correct). According to Wolff, the best interests of long-term viability and success required that this new ballpark should be situated fifty miles south of Oakland in San Jose (incorrect, if you ask most A's fans). If Wolff intended to establish rapport with fans, he was off to a terrible start.

The situation never improved and in the decade to follow, sensitive types might say that Wolff took potshots at the fans at every opportunity in order to illustrate that baseball in Oakland was unsustainable. During the lead up to the 2013 postseason, Wolff commented that the small attendance figures were depressing and that players approached him to express their sympathies for his predicament. Meanwhile, every other stadium new and old saw frequent renovations and overhauls, while the Coliseum sat there like a cement sarcophagus. Retrofitted to accommodate the return of the National Football League's Raiders from Los Angeles, the Coliseum now looks like a football stadium retrofitted to accommodate baseball. That's to say nothing of the annual national embarrassment when the inner workings of the stadium fail to keep sewage from overflowing into the bathrooms, clubhouses, and locker rooms. Aside from watching a terrific and exciting product on the field, the Coliseum offers little for fans. At its worst, the stadium serves as a constant reminder to long-suffering diehards that their ballpark is inadequate and the solution presented by ownership rests in an entirely different part of the state. I suppose it could be worse – at least the whispers of contraction have ceased, though relocation remains a scary alternative to "Plan A" in San Jose.

"There is a psychological trauma that fans go through when you have a fear of your team being contracted," Ricard said. "That's something we [Marlins fans] were faced with. There's a very strong psychological trauma that fans have to come to grips with. How do you root for something where the van is backing up and moving out? Even in Oakland – in that situation, you don't even care what the solution is. If it's like, 'We'll play on a cruise ship every weekend,' you'll say, 'Yeah, fine, I'll take it.' At least they'll be in town."

6

FANS AND HUMAN NATURE

June in the Midwest calls to mind visions of comfortable weather, sunshine, and the sounds of mitts popping and bats cracking from Chicago to St. Louis and back again. However, in the early days of the summer of 2010, the people of Chicago and the surrounding area were not quite ready to let the ice melt. On an early summer night in June, the Chicago Blackhawks were about to capture their fourth Stanley Cup, and they would do so in dramatic fashion.

With the score knotted at three apiece at the end of regulation, the Blackhawks and Eastern Conference Champion Philadelphia Flyers traded blows evenly for the first four minutes into a sudden death overtime period. Then, with just 54 seconds left to play in the first extra frame, Patrick Kane slipped a shot past goaltender Michael Leighton to lay claim to the National Hockey League's grandest prize. As Kane and teammate Patrick Sharp, a former Flyers farmhand, raised their hands in victory, the entire region surged into euphoric imitation. Across the Midwest, arms raised toward the sky, feet launched off the ground and the walls shook in every bar across Blackhawks Country.

Gabriel Torres, slapping hands and grinning ear-to-ear in the reflective glow of Blackhawks glory, celebrated in Washington, D.C. with his fellow Blackhawks Nation transplants on that June night. Torres, a dyed-in-the-wool Blackhawks fan, also happens to be a political anthropologist and faculty member at the University of Notre Dame. In this role, he has a unique perspective on why he – a Puerto Rican immigrant without much exposure to hockey or ice in general – might find himself intensely moved by the success of Chicago's hockey franchise. "Our nature is our propensity to have groups. And one of the evolutionary offshoots of that is the development of culture," Torres said. "Our sharing of belief and ideas is what helps us be group animals."

Torres began researching the anthropology of sports half a decade ago and quickly latched onto the sport of boxing. The interesting wrinkle with regard to research in the field of cultural anthropology is that it is quite unlike the research you might expect from your own college professors and other academic types. To better understand the boxing experience and get inside the minds of the men who choose to fight for sport and profession, Torres laced up the gloves, popped in a mouth guard, and started swinging. Taking on an apprenticeship as a trainer in South Bend, Indiana, he worked his way up the chain as an amateur and even made it into the professional ranks. Torres literally drew blood in the name of research. Cultural anthropologists like Torres believe that to understand fully what drives athletes to compete you must walk a mile in their shoes. Or in Torres' case, throw a few punches in their gloves. More importantly, and perhaps only possible by becoming his own subject, Torres learned that the genesis of individual boxing styles is rooted much deeper than pure personal preference, coaching or body type. Rather, it's a matter of race and nationality – in boxing, fighting styles are very much connected to cultural differences. You can see this culture-driven sporting style play out in other sports as well. Look no further than baseball. On the surface, every batting stance appears different and uniquely personal. Take a closer look at the plate approach of Japanese hitters and you will start to notice commonalities that are not often apparent in Western athletes. At the plate, many Japanese batters appear to swing and step toward first base in a single forward motion. Think Ichiro. Think Nori Aoki. This batting style, while not universally adopted by Japanese players, is still prevalent and noticeable in Japanese pro ball. Similarly, Latin American players come under fire at least once or twice each season for showboating at the plate and on the mound – the World Baseball Classic in 2013, for example, featured some of that flair. That year, everyone had an opinion about the Dominican Republic team, equal parts entertaining and polarizing, that ran roughshod through Major League Baseball's international tournament. The team gained as much recognition for their hot-dogging style as they did for being an utterly dominant ball club, which they were. Did showboating, creative victory celebrations, and sideways ball caps "disrespect" the game of baseball? Some people felt that way. I think it is difficult to judge the right and wrong way to play a game if you haven't had the opportunity to experience how the game is played outside of what you might be accustomed to in your home country. The Dominican team drew outside of the lines a bit, but it sure seemed like they were having more fun than anyone else throughout the competition. Winning played a role, but the Dominican team also seemed to enjoy one another's company. As Torres would explain to me, while we as a human species living in contemporary society tend to think of ourselves as individualistic, rational decision makers, "even the most individualistic of individuals are following patterns. Fundamentally, we are group people.

It's kind of what we've always done; that is our biology. So in that sense, that's the very foundation [of being human]."

If ever you were looking for a group to spend three hours celebrating shared passions, ideals, and culture with – regardless of how those paths might diverge in the day's other 21 hours – finding a local sports team to root for would be just the thing you needed. In sports, personal backgrounds and life situations matter little once the action starts. Draped in your chosen colors and with several thousand pairs of eyes trained in the same direction, sports fans are part of something beyond themselves, and that group experience can be addicting.

"We don't have many skating rinks in Puerto Rico, and by many I mean none," Torres said with a laugh, underscoring the unlikelihood of this marriage between fan and team. "I have some friends [and] neighbors that like hockey [and watching games together] was a good way to socialize. It was a good way to bring my own sense of community together in a place where it's hard to find community.

"Especially university communities, people come from all over the country and professors get hired from all over the place – they're international. Sometimes you have to find a way to tie yourself to a place. My love for Blackhawks hockey right now is serious; it's real. I go to the games, I share with fans, [and] I can connect and do the 'community thing' with the Blackhawk fans."

If the idea of "tying yourself to a place" sounds familiar, it's because that concept of community and team identification was central to John Ricard's story of life as a Marlins fan. For all of our differences as a species, the sports world brings people together against the backdrop of a shared interest. That interest can very quickly evolve into a little army of chanting and cheering bleacher creatures who, aside from their rooting interest, probably have more differences between one another than commonalities. Dr. Sam Sommers, the Tufts University psychology professor, mentioned that at its core, developing a rooting interest for a sports team is no different from becoming deeply involved in the world of Disney. He wondered why being a sports fan, abundant as we may be, does not carry the same esteem than being a fan of classical music or attending the opera as an extracurricular pursuit. Yet as I study the rituals of diehard sports fans, and with all due respect to Sommers, I started to find that the sports world is unique. The sports world rests outside the spectrum of other areas of interest – even when people with similar interests find one another. Indeed, as a fan of the opera, you might be pleasantly surprised to run into another individual with the same passion at a cocktail party. What a great conversation! The chance encounter could lead to lengthy discussions about recent visits to the Opera House, comparing notes regarding brilliant performances and perhaps even making plans to enjoy the opera together. Newly minted friends, bound by a common interest, are excited to have stumbled upon one another. I can see how these bonds that sports fans share with one another can translate to other areas of life to a degree. There are differences, however, that set sports fandom apart. There exists in every arena, bar, stadium, or living room a physicality unlike any that you might experience in day-to-day life or in any pursuit perhaps outside of religion. Even then, the physicality found in religion tends to be more subdued than what you might find in a packed arena. We will revisit the connection between sports and religion again a bit later. As I imagined Disney fanatics chest bumping, chanting, and high-fiving throughout the Magic Kingdom, Torres provided a bit more ammo for my hypothesis that the hand-slapping, lose-your-voice-from-cheering experience is unique to sports.

When studying human nature, Torres says, anthropologists often look to primates for glimpses into our evolutionary past. This area of focus, comparative primatology, can tell us a great deal about humankind. Humans and primates exhibit so many similarities with regard to our interactions with other members of our species that by studying the latter, we can learn more about our nature as human beings. "If you look at comparative primatology, you often see how important physicality is in building community," Torres said. "And think about it, there is a lot of physicality involved [in being a sports fan]."

If you were to compare levels of physicality, you might put sexual encounters at one extreme and perhaps a college lecture at the other end. For all of the boxing matches in his own research, I would imagine Torres' lectures at Notre Dame might be a bit less strenuous. Taking a few steps away from sex toward more public activities, consider for a moment the similarities between religious services, a packed dance club and a stadium filled with 45,000 screaming sports fans. According to Torres, these activities have a few things in common, and all serve as prime examples of communities strengthened through an abundance of physical interactions. "There's the issue of proximity or movements: alteration, jumping, high-fiving, and people bumping into each other. People will do things in those venues that you wouldn't do ordinarily. You wouldn't just be walking down the street with friends and start reacting like you would in a club, a stadium, or clearly during sex," Torres paused. "Well, you could, but you might get arrested. What they have in common is that they are places that have been set apart for humans to come together and physically enjoy themselves."

Fr. Jim Greanias, the Greek Orthodox priest who came under scrutiny for blessing the Chicago Cubs dugout, had expressed to me some months earlier his perspective on the differences between religious and fan experiences. From an anthropological viewpoint, however, thousands of years of human existence show that religion and sports are not as different as they may seem. Greanias' religious experience – the unexplained encounter that could only be from God – may differ from the euphoria associated with sports, but the lines blur with regard to rituals. Similarities abound. Sports and religion both serve to bring like-minded people together in a celebration of oneness and community. Regardless of denomination or belief system, religious experience centers on glorifying a God or gods. In sports, our energy as fans focuses squarely on the field of play where we venerate and honor the particular athletes donning our chosen colors. In both cases, we sit, stand, and chant at specific intervals – often on command. Holding hands and reciting the Lord's Prayer in unison during a Roman Catholic Mass becomes *"EVERY-BODY CLAP YOUR HANDS,"* the command to a congregation of sports fans in the form of cartoon hands banging together on an oversized scoreboard.

"You can play around with the idea that this [sports] is a religious experience. But maybe religion is a sports-like experience? I don't see any good reason to delineate it," Torres said as I quietly hoped I could someday host a debate between Torres and Greanias. "The best evidence for not drawing up these lines is that for much of early civilization – and by civilization I mean advanced state societies with agriculture and so on – we find that sports and religion were indeed one and the same. In the arenas, there were offerings to gods, and going to the arena was part of going to church. People often go to church for the same reasons they go to the stadium. Many theologies describe the ideal church community the same way people talk about the ideal fan community."

Sacred texts and hallowed grounds. You could be talking about Sunday church service or Sunday's Seventh Inning Stretch. I sound like a broken record when I take friends to Athletics games, because whenever one particular video hits the Coliseum scoreboard, I always say, "Oh, this one is my favorite." The video in question is a short film that blends moments from throughout the A's history in Oakland with recent memories made by the players of today. Yes, I'll admit it: I am a baseball nerd. However, for anyone with respect for baseball's past, its beauty is undeniable. That history, preserved and re-lived at each home game, is not unlike the passages shared during a church service. When Torres settles in to watch his beloved Chicago Blackhawks on Wednesday nights – Rivalry Night in the NHL – he hears the announcers recount the history of that evening's matchup. In sports, the history of our team serves as its sacred text and we cherish every word. Similarly, when Torres' Hawks take the ice at United Center, he tells me that the crowd is reminded of the monumental victories and intense battles on that icy surface. *This arena has seen some of the sport's greatest rivalries*, the announcer might exclaim. Again, we're reminded that this is hallowed ground where our heroes on skates go to war. In church, we shake hands and offer peace. At the arena, we slap hands and scream.

For every monumental victory, of course, there is an agonizing defeat. Even worse, sports can leave you with the distinct feeling that the team you love doesn't love you back with quite the same vigor. Ricard referred to it, aptly, as "psychological trauma" and compared the experience to that of a father who abandons his family for a younger, more attractive mistress. These are dramatic comparisons, but they speak volumes about how much love and devotion diehard fans pour into their teams. I wondered if there were any clues in our makeup as human beings that might explain these peculiarities. First, our fascination with sports overall and second, why we continue to care so deeply when so often we end up with disappointment and despair. In those moments, why do we continue to subject ourselves to the torment?

"It's the same reason why people persist in relationships that are not working out," Torres explained. "Look, I think the answer is the idea that you could possibly experience that moment of greatness. That euphoria is not much different from the ecstasy of a man and a woman or a man and a man, or whatever, in a relationship. You come together and experience this very intimate moment. In a relationship, it's usually sex. And in a sports venue it's winning the moment. The physiological reaction is not much different. You take some basic parameters like heartbeat alteration, and how you experience the pleasure of winning and the physicality of the moment are very similar."

Torres offered an eerie comparison between human relationships and our relationship with sports. In short, diehard sports fans are the needy ex-boyfriends of the sports world. He's not wrong: there are some incredible similarities with regard to our reaction to good and bad moments. Similar to how people react in different ways to break ups – meaning, some people are affected for a short period and then they move on, while others go into full-on stalker mode and are unable to cope for months or even years – fans react differently to sports performances depending on their level of attachment. The more invested the diehard fan is in his chosen team, the more intense his reaction might be to positive or negative outcomes in the sporting arena. These fans will hang on every pitch because they are deeply in tune with the realization that the moment of greatness can come at any time. In contrast, a casual fan might tune out for a couple innings because he or she is detached from the action. Sporting events entertain and when the show is over, casual fans can easily transition to the next activity on the agenda.

"I think the caring [about teams] is the same thing you see in the way people react to their relationships – you see the same sort of range among sports fans. You see the same sort of mourning for group affection and that group feeling [that comes with] scoring a goal all the way to winning the championship. People react to that differently and ultimately what they're seeking is the pleasure. Some people get that pleasure every time they score; you've seen that guy in the arena who is high-fiving way too much. And there's that guy who is always looking for that pleasure, that acknowledgment from other people," Torres said. "There are moments when hardly anyone in the arena can contain themselves, right? So whatever it is that we're looking for, that's ultimately what brings us back – that has to be it. What else could it be?"

Sports fans offer anthropologists like Torres, along with other researchers of the human experience, a terrific subject for study. Most research involves a control group and its counter experimental group. Sports, with its smaller subset of diehard fanatics, offer observers of human nature a vast swath of individuals of different ages, races, and political affiliations – just about every cross-section of society, really. In this way, researchers can draw stronger conclusions about why we do what we do and, with regard to sports fans, why we care so much about games. What inspires fans differs, but Torres reasons that the foundational driver for sports fans is a simple one: "Hey, this is fun and we want more fun. We want this pleasure. I think that's basically what it comes down to."

Rest assured, we will address fan violence in these pages before you reach the final chapter. Torres' conclusion that "sports are fun and we want to have fun" does not cover every dark corner of the world of sports fandom.

Rather, he speaks of the evolution of diehard fans and in a general sense, we are indeed having a hell of a lot of fun and we are enjoying ourselves in the company of people we like – people much like ourselves, even if we share no other common interests outside of the ballpark. That said, yes, there are rotten apples in the bushel. There are darker reasons for attaching oneself to a sports club than simply a desire for fun. Growing up as a Phillies fan, and still to this day grappling with other people's perceptions about what that says about me, I am all too aware that some fans (across all sports and every professional team, mind you) make bad decisions. If I never hear another word about Philadelphia sports fans booing Santa Claus or pelting a top draft pick that never signed with the team, J.D. Drew, with batteries, it will be too soon. Yes, fans do stupid things. Fans do even more stupid things when alcohol is involved, as it tends to be when aforementioned stupidity plays itself out within the context of sports.

That said, violent behavior connects itself to die-hard fandom for more complex reasons too. In parts of the world outside of our refined first-world fan experi-ences, political motivations and economics can frequently become entangled with sports. To that end, Torres assured me that despite similarities in how the global fan commu-nity approaches games (chanting, cheering, booing, and groaning), the reasons – communal, political, economic, or otherwise – he became attached to Blackhawks fandom nearly a decade ago differed considerably from those of, say, Serbian soccer fans in the early 1990s.

They say that familiarity breeds contempt and that's as likely to be true in the sports world as in any other sphere. Consider the greatest rivalries in athletics and the common denominators often include a similar combination of fac-tors. These include, but are not limited to, proximity of location, frequency of match-ups and, perhaps the most important factor all, that the two opposing forces are competitive during the same period. You can make the argument that Red Sox and Yankees fans will always boo and hiss at one another relentlessly regardless of where they sit in the standings. However, in most cases, rivalries reach their boiling point when the games mean something. Add deep-seated and opposing political beliefs and an extreme level of prejudice and you have a lethal cocktail better known today as the Soccer Wars.

In 1990, Red Star Belgrade and Dinamo Zagreb were among the top clubs in the Yugoslav Football League. Like most sports franchises, both teams had a massive army of boosters and fan groups. The difference during this period of world history is that a portion of Red Star supporters, the Delije, represented ultranationalist Serbian interests while Dinamo Zagreb fans supported Croatian independence. For league organizers, the cards fell the wrong way when these two matched up a few short weeks following the first multi-party election in more than 50 years for Croatia. In that election, parties favoring Croatian independence won majority votes, led by new President Franjo Tudjman. This did not go over well with the Dilije and its ruthless leader, Arkan. History shows too that Arkan would later recruit the most vicious of Serbian nationalists to join his crusade of ethnic cleansing of Croats and Muslims. He was ultimately assassinated just before going on trial for said massacres. But on that day in 1990 when Red Star Belgrade and Dinamo Zagreb went head-to-head, Arkan and his anti-Croat, anti-Muslim platform were very much alive. Led by opposing forces of soccer hooligans with an unhealthy dose of national pride, supporters of both teams clashed in a big way. These were not your run-of-the-mill soccer hooligans raging at the local pub and chanting with pride for their club of choice. As Red Star Belgrade and Dinamo Zagreb prepared for battle on the pitch, fans literally went to war in the seats. More than 60 fans suffered injuries amid the fury heightened by significant political overtones in what many Croatians considered the symbolic start of the Croatian War of Independence.

"That's an extreme example, but it's not unique. In Spain, [Francisco] Franco's team was Real Madrid. To this day many people identify Real Madrid as a fascist team, which is kind of a stretch, of course, because that team has become something else," Torres said. "At the same time, if you're cheering for Real Madrid in the latter part of the 20th century, you were probably politically allied to the Franco regime. There are nationalistic undertones." This – the Soccer Wars, Spanish dictators and fascist football clubs – brings us all the way back to where we started: the attempt to understand what could possibly cause a Puerto Rican immigrant to root for 23 men on skates donning the image of a Native American in war paint and feathers emblazoned on their chest.

"I remember [that] I was in D.C. when they [Chicago Blackhawks] won the championship and I went to Buffalo Billiards, a DuPont Circle bar," Torres recalled. "The mechanism that underlies my ability to cheer and invest so much emotion in Blackhawks hockey ... I can tell you where I was and what I was wearing, but I don't know who was there – I can't tell you the names of who was there, but there was a lot of community sharing during that game that was great. The mechanisms there might be the very same as in Serbia and Madrid with the soccer clubs, but the reasons why we come together to cheer like that differ."

Human beings do not have a predisposition toward becoming sports fans. We are not guided toward fandom by the pull of rituals and routines set forth by our ancestors thousands of years ago. Humans are, however, driven by the desire to be with others. It is human nature to seek community and the act of gathering, sharing, and socializing is, for most people, among the more desirable outputs from our short time on Earth. Torres, whether cheering for the Blackhawks with his neighbors or with strangers in a packed bar, had been drawn to the team as the happy conclusion to his search to find his place in, and connect with, a strange new city. His was a search to find a real connection with people in the artificial and transient university environment. This motivation to be part of something and to socialize might be the very same stimulus that lured fans to Franco's Real Madrid, Arkan's Delije, or Dinamo Zagreb, the symbol of Croatian independence. Of course, cultural circumstances and context matter. Nationalistic undertones, political disorder, and extraordinary economic conditions can transform sports fandom into something quite different. At its core, however, is our tendency to associate with others and sport, for better or worse, is well-suited to provide the payoff we seek as human beings. It's only natural.

7
EVOLUTION OF A SUPER FAN

Chip Hale leaned back with his arms crossed and head tilted to the side to watch the action in front of him while also engaging in conversation with a man seated just behind him. Hale, a modestly successful ballplayer across nine big league seasons with the Los Angeles Dodgers and Minnesota Twins, has ascended to a higher echelon of esteem in his second career as a coach. In this instance, he sat hidden in plain sight while scouting a Single-A game as the Bench Coach for the Oakland Athletics. During his tenure in Oakland, many throughout the pro circuit believed Hale would get his shot at managing at the Major League level in due course. More than a few cocked an eyebrow when the Seattle Mariners, a frontrunner to make Hale a first-time manager, passed him up just before the 2014 season to select another first-timer, Lloyd McClendon. Shortly after the 2014 season, however, the Arizona Diamondbacks anointed Hale its next manager and gave him the chance to turn a struggling club around under the watchful eyes of baseball royalty in the form of General Manager Dave Stewart and Chief Baseball Officer and Major League Baseball Hall of Famer Tony LaRussa. That's quite a turn of events for a man who had spent his playing days and early coaching career as a relative unknown. But while athletic skills deteriorate with age, a sharp mind has incredible staying power. Hale remains a constant reminder that there will always be a place for intelligent baseball minds at the big league level regardless of past on-field exploits.

On this day in early June, a day off for his employer, Hale sits directly behind home plate within the cozy dimensions of San Jose Municipal Stadium watching the Stockton Ports pay visit to the San Jose Giants. The over-sized advertisements draped from corner to corner of the outfield wall offer a faint reminder of a past era when big leaguers played in front of enormous outfield advertise-ments that screamed out from 400-plus feet away. Back then, it was always LIFEBOY and BULOVA, demanding attention from afar. But make no mistake about it: we are not in the big leagues on this cool night in June. The Ports, as the A's Advanced Single-A squad, are comprised of a few promising first-round draft picks and a handful of 20-somethings whose big league journey may very well end here in the low minors. These young men are trying to refine their craft and take the next step, which for some, never comes. Tonight, while competing against a team of Giants farmhands also trying to keep the big league dream alive, they are also competing for the eye of Hale and a host of scouts speckled anonymously throughout the stands. Regardless of their performance, they can always count on the attention – and support – of one man. Perched above the right ear of future major league manager Chip Hale, he has himself drawn the attention of the most important man in the ballpark.

"Chip [Hale] is a really good guy. He's one of my – we're extremely close," Will MacNeil stopped short of calling Hale one of his best friends. At least, that's what it sounded like he was about to say. Okay, that probably wasn't what he was going to say at all. However, after spending a few hours with MacNeil and hearing his stories of life as an Athletics super fan, I wouldn't be a bit surprised. I also wouldn't be surprised to learn that the feeling was mutual because to this point of our new friendship, first impressions of MacNeil are already forming. He is incredibly endearing.

MacNeil was nice enough to donate a few hours of his time to my cause – namely, writing a book about why people like MacNeil feel the way they do about sports. After careful consideration of our social agendas (mine involving tending to my wife and child and his focused on balancing work with plans to see live baseball once or twice each day), we determined that a Ports game in San Jose was just what the doctor ordered for both of us. While he is not a household name, if you have been to an Athletics game and cast your gaze to right field, you can't miss him. He's the jersey-clad diehard waving flags, singing songs, and supporting his team with every fiber of his being. He's the fan who shows up on ESPN highlights when the national sports network decides to focus on Oakland baseball. His section, 149, is responsible for such oddities as Bacon Tuesday (where fans bring every imaginative bacon creation they can get their hands on into the stands). Furthermore, MacNeil and the right field bleacher crew have formed unlikely bonds with opposing players like Jeff Francoeur, Josh Hamilton, and L.J. Hoes. MacNeil himself, however, is responsible for what turned out to be a stadium-wide solute to former A's closer Grant Balfour: the Balfour Rage.

"The Balfour Rage was the most surreal thing in the world," he said. "I never did that to try to get any recognition. We were so bad in 2011 that I was just trying to be funny with my friends, and then game 162 in 2012 [the day the A's overtook Texas to win the AL West] and that thing took off and everyone in the stadium was doing that. I was like, 'Wow, I started a trend. This is actually really

scary that this thing took off like it did.' It was really surreal that that happened."

As a communications executive in my regular life
outside of the ballpark, I wish there was a way to bottle
up some of that creative genius emanating from diehards
across the sports arena. From the Yankee Stadium roll
call (led by diehard Bald Vinny, the bleacher creatures at
Yankee Stadium cheer for each member of the Yankees
starting lineup until the supported player acknowledges
the attention) to MacNeil's mosh pit-worthy fists of
Balfour Rage, front office marketers have often attempted
to repeat the viral nature of these phenomena. As of this
writing, they have yet to crack the code. There's just something that grabs you when you watch a fan-created trend
flowing out from every corner of the stadium. The sensation differs greatly from the mechanical direction coming
at you from the team, demanding that you CLAP YOUR
HANDS or MAKE NOISE. No thank you, I'll take my cues
from my community of fellow diehards if you don't mind.

"One year we had a 'Chicken Thursday' where we
all just brought loads of different kinds of chicken like
Popeye's, Buffalo, and everything," MacNeil said, confirming that Bacon Tuesday is but one of the many
food-focused themes dreamed up by his bleacher family.
"With the head-banging [when Athletics' closer Sean
Doolittle enters the game], all that stuff is organic. People
told me I had to come up with something for [former
Athletics pitcher] Jim Johnson and nothing clicked
because there was almost more pressure. The Balfour
thing happened because I was having a good time goof-
ing around. Everyone started laughing at me, but then it
slowly took off."

In San Jose, our conversation is often stopped short
because we are not just talking – we are invested deeply
in a ball game. We are supporting the visitors here at

Municipal Stadium, so when third baseman Renato Nunez lines a shot in the gap for the Ports' first hit of the night in the second inning, it's time to make some noise. "Two! Two! Two! Hold! Hold!" MacNeil has shot himself right out of our conversation and into the dugout alongside the baby-faced farmhands, shouting orders to the kid standing safely on second base. He may as well be a coach, actually, with how well he knows the players and coaches and, in turn, how well they all seem to know him. And man, I'm not sure I've met anyone else offering as much positive energy and encouragement before in my life. "Nice contact, Bruce! Way to get him over to third," he exclaimed while applauding aggressively. The team's top catching prospect peeked up and nodded to MacNeil as he sauntered back to the dugout after a meek groundout to first moved Nunez up one station along the base paths with two outs in the inning. Another groundout, this time by Dusty Robinson, stranded Nunez at second and ended the frame. "You the man, Dusty!"

MacNeil is on a first-name basis with just about everyone inside any A's affiliate within driving distance. While technically a front desk attendant at a Bay Area chain hotel, MacNeil's real job comes from a place of passion. Chief among the primary responsibilities of this second job includes trying to figure out how to fill his calendar with as much professional and amateur baseball as possible while continuing to work enough shifts at his hotel to remain employed. Sometimes, that means working overnight graveyard shifts and, on the rarest of occasions, it means he has to miss one of his beloved A's games. The graveyard shifts in particular are a real trip, as they're typically bookended by two two-a-days. Athletes, particularly those in the NFL during the sweltering summer training camp months, are familiar with the concept of two-a-days: that grueling regimen involving both a morning and afternoon workout. MacNeil's gauntlet is similarly taxing, though it offers a different type of endurance training. He consults the schedules of every Athletics affiliate and independent league team within driving distance and zeroes in on two that pass the feasibility test. What is this test, you ask? There is but one question: can I get from one park to the other by first pitch of the second game? Should he find but one workable game on the pro circuit, MacNeil turns his attention to a cadre of independent and college teams at play across the San Francisco Bay Area on any given night to lock in that number two spot on the calendar. In doing this, he can take in an afternoon and evening game in two different cities – often no closer than 40 miles apart. After a day of refueling on baseball, he works all night, grabs an hour or two of sleep once his shift ends and then does it all again. Tonight is an easy night: a trip to San Jose is the only game on the agenda.

"The funniest thing I did this year was an independent doubleheader," he explained as we discussed the two-a-day grind. If you're unfamiliar with the Independent Leagues, it's typically a proving ground for washed up former big leaguers looking to get back to the spotlight mixed in with a bunch of ballplayers hoping for their first shot at catching on with a minor league team. The quality of play can at times be an absolute delight, or it could be disgraceful to the game of baseball. "San Rafael played Sonoma and then I went home for just a few minutes, and then I went all the way out to Pittsburg to see Pittsburg play Vallejo. I did an independent doubleheader and a lot of people [laughed about it], but it was 18 innings of good independent ball, and I loved it."

On the field in front of us, a lawn not quite on par with the palatial landscape primped and preened by the talented groundskeepers of its parent club, the bats are as cold as the surprisingly chilly evening breeze. The Ports batters spend a frustrating evening scorching the ball on the screws, but also directly at the hometown Giants fielders. We are watching Single-A ball, however, and the Giants would stumble into enough mistakes to keep the youngsters from the visiting squad in the game until the bitter end. Case in point: a line drive off the bat of Giants first baseman Brian Ragira split the gap between center field and right. An easy trot home for the lead runner at second base, unless he loses track of the ball's path in the outfield. A rare occurrence, of course. Tonight? The lead runner failed to score because he lost track of the ball's path into the outfield. The ball, hit well, not only landed between the two Ports outfielders, but also rolled all the way to the wall and should have doubled the lead. The Giants did manage to save a little face and run the score up to 3-0 before the end of the inning. However, a base-running blunder – common in these always-learning depths of minor league ball – limited the damage and kept the Ports within striking distance.

Such is life outside of The Show. And MacNeil loves every minute of it. "I should go back and count them up," he says, when I ask how many games he had been to here in the early summer months. "I would have to say ... at least 70, maybe 80."

Just then, the Giants' mascot Gigante strolls through and gestures toward the visiting super-fan. The mascot stares in, points at Will and flashes the thumbs down signal. "Go Ports!" MacNeil barks back to Gigante, a mascot that, I must say, looks a bit crudely stitched together. I'm surprised less by the interaction with MacNeil and more by the fact that approaching children are not trembling in fear as they get closer to the towering gargoyle-looking weirdo. While not quite the closet of horrors found in most seasonal Halloween costume stores, we'll just say that for all of his fan-friendly interactions with doting fans, Gigante lacks the polished look of his Major League counterparts. "We've still got more rings than you!" Ah, the parting shot from MacNeil. Gigante throws his head back as if his back has just given out. MacNeil possesses such detailed knowledge of the history and accomplishments of every minor league team that might stand in the way of his own. Gigante approaches, the two shake hands. As mascots are wont to do, Gigante locks MacNeil into a playful headlock. The hometown mascot gets the upperhand, much to the amusement of the hometown crowd and even a friendly pat on the back from his opponent. *Well played - you got me this time!* The two part ways, but I'm altogether surprised at how much time this mascot spends harassing our hero throughout the game. I suppose with a crowd of 2,500 – mostly donning home team colors – the dissenting faction in head-to-toe Ports blue sticks out like a sore thumb. Enough with the frivolities. There's a game to win tonight, so MacNeil turns his attention back to the action just as the Ports' batter receives a gift call from home plate umpire Malachi Moore. "Ooh, thank you blue," he says. His sentiment is, of course, an improvement over the barbs he had sent toward Moore earlier in the game when he shouted out, "Let's actually have a good strike zone today, Malachi!" Few fans know the Single-A umpiring rotation by name like MacNeil. In this instance, I'm sure Moore, learning on the job in the low levels of minor league ball, would rather fly beneath the radar. The daggers cut deep at times, even if tossed in good, clean fun. MacNeil admitted as much, mentioning that after referring to an umpire as a midget and getting carried away with his heckling one night in Stockton, the home plate umpire actually tossed him out of the game. That's the extent of the umpire's power between the lines, but apparently it can extend into the grandstands when necessary. Lesson learned.

That being said, the one thing they can all count on – the players, coaches, officials, mascots and fans alike – is that when it comes time to toss the game's first pitch, Will MacNeil will be there more often than not.

"Baseball is one of those sports where all year it never leaves my thought process. I'm on baseball all year," he shared with me during our second meeting a few months later at his go-to sports bar in San Leandro, California. That our second talk came three months after the first was no accident. After weeks of trying to connect for a sit-down interview – away from the ballpark and its many distractions – I soon realized that it's difficult to pin this man down during the baseball season. If he's not sitting in the right field bleachers – section 149, row 27 (actual first row), seat 7, home away from home for the past nine years – he's on the road to one Bay Area park or another. So yes, this mid-September follow-up meeting required a stroke of strategic planning on my part, as I waited for all minor and independent league seasons to end and for the Athletics to have an off day. It took three months, but on this night, we had all the time in the world to sip beers and talk baseball. "I've only missed maybe six games all year, but even those games I miss, I'm actually on edge to be there. I need to be there," MacNeil said. "There's a major component of my life missing, which makes me realize that I need to grow up if I feel that way."

Maybe. In his early thirties, living on his own and trying to make ends meet, MacNeil believes it might be time to "grow up" and stop feeding his insatiable addiction to baseball. Doing so, however, would serve as a betrayal of the great connector that has added such richness to his life. Through baseball, MacNeil has established deep and lasting friendships with the fellow diehards he has spent his summers with year-in and year-out for the better part of a decade. Through baseball, he has established professional connections that could still one day lead him out from behind the reception desk and into the world of amateur scouting. A career path in baseball is not the pipe dream of a star-crossed optimist. On the contrary, of his dear friend Chip Hale, MacNeil tells me, "He loves the fact that I go to Stockton. He asks me for scouting reports – scout Daniel Robertson, scout so-and-so. And I tell him, he has a swing like this, he did this and this and this in the field, and so he appreciates it." He's even found romance and, thankfully, his girlfriend enjoys the game almost as much as he does. Most of all, however, MacNeil has found a home in the cavernous confines of the Coliseum and, more specifically, the right field bleachers.

"That ballpark is home. People call that ballpark a dump, but it's our dump. It's a place where there's so much history and I have so many great memories of everybody I've sat with through the years," he explained. "I keep going every day because of my friends; it's almost like a family – it's like my summer family. We even do stuff in the offseason. We're just a very close group of friends, and we share a love of baseball and that's how we all got to know each other and that's the best thing in the world. Nothing will ever replace being out there with those 20 to 30 people I'm with on a nightly basis. Nothing could ever replace that."

MacNeil waves his green and gold flag (donning the label "RF Will 149") in rhythmic timing with a handful of other flag-wavers. Each season, his best friends surround him on the right side of his beloved Athletics' Oakland home. But as we've discovered at this point, those friendships in and through baseball are not limited to the people on his left, right and directly behind him in the stands. Rather, MacNeil has endeared himself to the athletes and their leaders who traipse along the lush grasslands a few feet in front of him as well. While we kick back at the bar, he shares a few stories of people in the game that he has become friendly with through the years. He recounted the offseason phone calls with former Athletics Minor League Pitcher of the Year, Dan Straily, whose 2014 trade to the Chicago Cubs still stings for MacNeil even with the passage of time. "It really hurt when he got traded. I still talk to him quite a bit. He's one of the good guys in the game." He told me of Oakland farmhand Seth Frankoff, a young man knocking at the door of the big leagues with a 2014 promotion to Triple-A ball. MacNeil has become friendly with Frankoff and his wife – both of whom look after him throughout the season. "[He] even gave me a few bucks for gas one game, and I was like, 'no, no, no!' I made sure to give it back to him, but one day I found it in the back of my pocket. He or his wife slipped it in and I didn't notice it, but they try to take care of me."

These friendships don't happen by accident. They happen because MacNeil, very much living the day-to-day struggle of life on a dime himself, has an appreciation for the daily grind of the modern day ballplayer toiling away in every level of minor league and independent ball. And that appreciation sticks out like a sore thumb. The teen and 20-something kids making their way toward the million-dollar dream of that big league payday bide their time bussing from city to city on a diet of Carl's Jr. and Top Ramen noodles. The life is not glamorous, and you know what? For MacNeil, logging thousands of miles from ballpark to ballpark – and sometimes, amateur field to amateur field – life is not glamorous. And even still, these athletes possessing either raw skill and potential or raw grit and determination to never give up the dream see him out there cheering his ass off, and the appreciation is mutual. Former Athletics Tommy Everidge and Bobby Cramer were among the first to recognize and welcome the energy and positivity MacNeil poured into their minor league performances. It was through their friendship that MacNeil's love of the game grew even stronger. "Those are two of the first players in the minor leagues I got to know really well. They would offer me tickets, would call me during the offseason and we would talk. They helped my love of minor league baseball grow and then when they made it to Oakland, it was almost like a family member made it," he explained, as a grin crept across his face. His tone changed to one of pride and satisfaction as he waxed nostalgic about two close friends who made it to the big leagues, even if only for a short time. "The thrill of seeing someone [that] you know who grinded it out in the minor leagues – the 'bus leagues' – especially Bobby Cramer. He was out of ball for a while, pitched in Mexico, and was a substitute teacher. And when he finally made it to the big leagues it was one of the biggest thrills in the world to see someone I knew finally get that chance. It's almost as if a family member made it."

Few fans enjoy that level of authentic closeness with professional athletes, and it's likely because of that reason that MacNeil endures his fair share of detractors. Yes, this super-positive, through-and-through diehard deals with an opposing force as if he were a high school kid picked on in the schoolyard by bullies. In an age where social networks like Twitter – his social vice of choice – leave us exposed to undue criticisms and anonymous attacks, such is life. MacNeil uses these platforms to channel positivity and maintain his connections to players, their wives and other pros in the game (right on down to the public address announcer for his beloved Stockton Ports). With that choice come the attacks – especially when the local squad underperforms, as it had been doing for a nearly 40-game stretch when we met that September night. Sadly, some of the barbs tossed his way are from his fellow bleacher diehards whose insults he brushes off with a dismissive refrain of, "Emo A's fans." That's his description of the hot-and-cold, over-emotional fans that forget what life was like in Oakland between 2007 and 2011 (read: it was not very good) when times were tough for the mostly successful ball club. When they start throwing daggers anyone preaching positivity, MacNeil – Mr. Positivity himself – falls squarely in their crosshairs.

"People tell me I'm a kiss ass because I'm friends with some of the players or the wives and I get called a lot of names for that, but people fail to realize that [from] 2007 to 2011 we were garbage. We were one of the worst teams in baseball year-in and year-out. Realize how good we have it that we're even in playoff contention," he said. I can't help but hear myself three years earlier as I listen to MacNeil. You see, the St. Louis Cardinals had just knocked the Phillies out of the 2011 postseason. While the Cardinals celebrated, first baseman Ryan Howard writhed in pain somewhere between home plate and first base with a torn Achilles tendon. Some 3,000 miles west, I sunk deep into my couch in the solitude of my San Francisco Bay Area home. This conclusion for the best team in baseball (the Phillies won 102 games that year – the most in their 125-plus year history) was sub-optimal. Watching on while far removed from the action, I felt an overwhelming sadness creep into my body. Moments later, I turned to Twitter and thanked the Phillies for a magical season. At that time, I found comfort in reprising the role of the lone positive voice in a sea of negativity. I took a deep breath and realized that in my lifetime, this could very well be the end of a five-year run of success – that included one World Series title and another World Series appearance, I might add – I had never known as a sports fan, let alone a long-suffering Phillies fan. Sure enough, the glory years had indeed ended with Howard's game-ending ground out and offseason appointment for tendon surgery. And the sadness? Oh boy, the sadness was real as can be. But I was sad because I know that playoff baseball is not a right – nothing is guaranteed. My team had missed a golden opportunity to capitalize on what had been the best 162-game stretch of baseball I had experienced in my entire lifetime. And in the end, they blew it. As I spoke with MacNeil that night at Ricky's Sports Bar, I realized he acknowledged the same basic truths of fandom. "Playoffs are a privilege. It's something that a lot of people don't realize.

"There are some nights where for about 15 to 30 minutes, I'm really ticked off; I'm upset as can be. But I just breathe, relax, and realize that there is other stuff in life that's a lot more important. Sometimes it's hard to realize that, but there's a lot of stuff that's more important so I just breathe, post a positive tweet to show my side of it and try to tell everybody it's going to be ok. If we make it [to the playoffs], great. If we don't there's going to be a lot of changes, but our team is going to still be around for a bit. Relax. It's going to be ok."

We're kicking back enjoying a night out, and as I carry on about my roots and learn about MacNeil's life as an Athletics diehard, I nearly forget that I'm here on a mission. Before we head our separate ways, I need to uncover the origin story of his green and gold obsession. I bear down and focus, because I know that there was indeed a day that this Oakland Athletics super-fan and baseball nut was not driving from Pittsburg to San Rafael for an independent league doubleheader. There was a day, or a moment, that captured his heart forever. That day will occupy a slice of real estate in his brain for as long as he's able to settle into seat seven in that first row of the Coliseum's section 149. Turns out, it all started with a muscle-bound slugger named Mark McGwire.

"First game I ever remember watching on TV. It was a road game in Minnesota and this guy by the name of Mark

McGwire came to the plate, and he just hits this bomb of a homerun and they're wearing these ugly softball-looking uniforms and I was just like, 'that's my team,'" he said. "I picked them right there as a three or four-year-old kid. I had a big foam bat in my hand I was trying to mimic his swing. I just fell in love with Mark McGwire and fell in love with the A's."

The fascination of an impressionable toddler has taken on a life of its own, of course. MacNeil estimates, at the time of our second conversation, that while he would likely fall short of his goal of attending 200 games in one season across countless iterations of the game of baseball, he would still manage somewhere in the 170 to 180 range. In fact, he was quick to remind me that he still had eight games on the docket for November. A road trip to check out the Arizona Fall League awaits on the horizon following the end of the big league season. That's when I started doing a little math. Knowing how much it was costing me to make it out to a significantly smaller percentage of games – and even that figure is enough to make my wife cringe – I couldn't begin to imagine the damage MacNeil's love affair with baseball was doing on his finances. An hourly employee who had already shared with me a few stories of minor league ballplayers helping him along the path toward 200 games with free tickets, gas money and other acts of kindness – baseball is an expensive game and MacNeil is managing the best he can. Needless to say, beers are on me on this night. So, how much of a financial burden is this children's game we love so much?

"I've never even thought about that," MacNeil said. My heart skipped a beat. I almost died as he uttered those words. "That's something honestly that doesn't even cross my mind. I try to ignore that because I mean, I buy so much beer, food, hats, jerseys ... that's why when Seth [Frankoff] made it to Sacramento [formerly the Athletics

Triple-A affiliate], that was huge because I only had to pay 10 bucks for parking. If I had an actual figure, I'd be really scared to see what it was. I try to ignore that aspect of it." I pressed. He delivered. "If I had to guesstimate a total, it's probably $10,000 at least and that's probably [underestimating] how much it probably really is." Heart in throat, I am speechless. And then, I remember MacNeil's words from earlier in the evening. This game has brought him immense joy. The friendships, love, and the satisfaction through the years keeps him coming back for more. Who am I to put a price on that? He finds a way every season to make it work. The question then is not whether the financial burden is going to be too much to overcome. Rather, is the grind going to be too much to overcome?

"I'll be very honest – I don't tell many people this. There are some days I realize I'm killing myself in a way," he said. "There are some nights I'm driving from Sacramento back to Pleasanton when I was living in Pleasanton where I'm almost dozing off because I'm just worn down because I worked in the morning and went to a Rivercats game and drove back and had to work the next morning.

"There are those moments when it's a burden, but I wouldn't trade it for the world. I realize that there's going to be some day I'm going to need to give this up. Next season, I won't be able to go to as many minor league games and that'll be the real test to see how I handle it. I'll either be fine or I'll be really trying to find a new identity or something – it may really hurt."

Our conversation shifted from one of his reality to that of the public perception of Oakland fans. In 2014, the Athletics surpassed the two million attendance mark for the first time since 2005, and just barely (2,003,628 to be exact). That's a weighty figure for an oft-ridiculed fan base whose conviction comes into question with every winning season paired with poor attendance figures. That

Detroit Tigers ace Justin Verlander, citing an intense and in-tune crowd, called the A's home ballpark the most difficult environment he had ever played in during the 2012 American League Divisional Series should serve as validation that Oakland loves its baseball team and knows the intricacies of the game. Sadly, the team is saddled with a bottom-third attendance total year after year and for the general baseball-viewing public, that's typically enough evidence to make broad assumptions about the team's fans. As a participant and first-hand observer, perception couldn't be further from the truth. As I sit with MacNeil, I can sense that it gnaws at him.

"There are some nights when there might be 12, 15-thousand or something and they [people looking in from outside] might think, 'oh, they don't really care.' But that 12 to 15-thousand A's crowd sounds like 45,000 because we have so much passion and we care so darn much for this team," MacNeil said. "I grind to pay for my $850 tickets [per seat, the cost for a full season in the bleachers] each year. I have to work my butt off to pay. I'm going to find a way to do it no matter what, but it may actually hurt me in the long run getting food or something. But I will pay for my tickets because I love this team almost more than anything."

8
FANS AND VIOLENCE

I remember the moment distinctly. I had just wrapped up a call with Dr. Schwartz, the cardiology fellow, to learn about his research on the health impacts of exciting sporting moments. Closing out the call, I asked, simply enough, if he had anything else to add before we went our separate ways. He used that time to turn me on to an independent study conducted by one of his peers that reviewed a few years of Sunday police activity in U.S. cities that host pro football teams. As he spoke, I felt as though I was hearing about a dirty little secret kept under wraps by America's most successful sports league. During that next part of our conversation, he shared that he had been subtly encouraged by his superiors to leave the study out of his own paper on sports fandom and health as to not arouse controversy. As he said this, I could feel the hair rise on the back of my neck and my voice waver as quiet panic set in. The all-powerful, invincible National Football League has a few skeletons in its closet and a few chinks in its armor. Times have changed, of course, since my conversation with Schwartz. The league proved to be imperfect and incapable of escaping controversy within its own ranks and unsure about how to react properly. Well-publicized domestic violence incidents among its player ranks revealed the ugly truth that the golden boys in the Commissioner's Office had no idea whatsoever about how to handle their misbehaving players. The missteps, backpedaling, half-truths and disingenuous post-outrage punishments made the NFL – the most popular professional sports league in America – look like a bunch of keystone cops. For all its might, the NFL failed its constituents by fumbling through the world's saddest and most futile attempt at self-preservation.

The scariest part of my 20-second exchange with Schwartz, however, was not that the NFL itself had done anything wrong. Rather, that the league, despite its strength and sway, could do nothing to stop this private nightmare from playing out in the homes of its broad fan base each week. Of course, as the world learned in the months leading up to and throughout an excruciating sideshow of the football season, the NFL is ill prepared to handle matters of the home even when its superstars are the savages throwing the punches.

Drs. David Card and Gordon Dahl tracked more than a decade of Sunday police reports in NFL cities with an eye toward instances of domestic violence. The research informed their study, "Family Violence and Football: The Effect of Unexpected Emotional Cues on Violent Behavior," which ran initially in *The Quarterly Journal of Economics* in 2009. Wins and losses in football, and one can assume all or most other sports, do not maintain a direct connection to increased instances of family violence. However, adding the element of the unexpected to an otherwise expected series of outcomes led to a startling hypothesis by Card and Dahl. Based on their research, upset losses – which the researchers qualified as losses by the home team despite expectations of a win by more than four points – led to a 10 percent increase in at-home violence between men and their wives or girlfriends in a short period following the game's conclusion. The study also concluded that upset wins, which in theory should have resulted in a broad swath of generally content fans, had little impact if any on instances of domestic violence following games. Meaning, the researchers noted similar police activity on a Sunday featuring an epic victory by the home team as they did on days when the point spread in Las Vegas predicted an easy win. In other words, if a man had any intention of attacking a loved one in the first place, feeling good about his favorite football team might cause him to pause for a moment, but it would not be enough to stop the violence from taking place eventually.

Card, a professor of economics at the University of California, Berkeley, explained to me that domestic violence has long been a puzzle to economists. That is because it is in direct conflict with how experts in the field of economics tend to view the innate purpose of the family unit. Economists believe the essential traits of the family unit are cooperation and protection. Therefore, domestic violence runs completely off the rails of expected behavior. According to Card, "we were interested in the idea that some faction of violence, maybe not all of it, but some faction of violence is a result of a situation flaring up and going out of control rather than some kind of well-planned victimization where a husband or a boyfriend systematically victimizes his partner for reasons of control."

Thus, a study of NFL fans emerged. Pro football presents researchers with a perfect environment for in-depth study due to many rhythmic, repeatable factors. The predictable nature of NFL schedules, astronomical local ratings for games, and immense media hype for each week's slate of gridiron match-ups allows for easy tracking of fluctuating data points. This predictability and popularity, in turn, drives quick-trigger emotional reactions and creates a perfect playground for researchers. Given the general isolation of NFL games to Sundays (with the occasional Thursday and single weekly Monday game) and the surprisingly accurate work of Las Vegas odds-makers, Card and Dahl were able to pinpoint the effect of game outcomes on family violence in a way that would be much more difficult in other sports. During the NFL season, most teams lock into competition on a single day. Because those games tend to begin and end at predictable intervals, tying unrelated activity to the extracurricular of sports fans becomes much easier than it would be otherwise. Therefore, when police activity spikes by 10 percent a few short hours after the highly favored home squad loses on Football Sunday, researchers like Card and Dahl take notice. "We showed that exactly in those situations where there's an unexpected loss, there's an elevation of calls to the police," Card said. "And there's a bunch of things that make that even a stronger effect [higher percentage of police call volume]. The strongest effect is when it's a high-stakes game – a game that might be decisive for the team going on in the season." Card also cited traditional rivalries as a key element of higher call volume when the favored team falls to its lesser foe.

We talked awhile about what the NFL could do to help prevent its fans from making horrible decisions following four quarters of football. Surely, the nation's most powerful sports organization could end the violence if it chose to acknowledge that some among its masses have difficulty controlling their emotions and actions beyond the playing field. I will admit that my first instinct upon hearing about the connection between football fans and domestic violence was to figure out a way to take the league to task for turning a blind eye to its black eye. This is a reasonable assumption considering how poorly the world's leading football association maintains control over the behavior of its own players. In 2014 alone, several players including superstar Baltimore Ravens running back Ray Rice spent the season tangled up in the league's own domestic violence scandal. Even with recent events, it's difficult to say that they have ignored the problem. The league partners with global brands in support of domestic violence prevention programs and its most valuable asset, the players, help dozens or even hundreds of organizations designed to educate and prevent. The more Card and I discussed the causes of the problem, the more I came to realize that the only real league-driven solution would be a concerted effort to tamp down fan excitement about its product. That, obviously, is never going to happen. An alternative, similarly unlikely option, might be throwing its might behind a campaign to limit the nation's alcohol consumption. "In a very large portion of these cases there's evidence that at least one of the parties involved was drinking," Card said. He also mentioned that historical police reports show that domestic violence calls spike on big drinking holidays like St. Patrick's Day and New Year's Eve, and that drinking is highly correlated with domestic violence. The crazy thing is that reducing violent incidents of all types at sporting events, according to sports psychologist Daniel Wann, may be as easy as limiting alcohol consumption at games. Unfortunately, there's just so much money wrapped up in beer sponsorships alone that it is unreasonable to expect that stadiums would suddenly stop selling alcohol, even if the resulting benefit is a reduction in violent occurrences.

"You take alcohol out of NFL stadiums and the number of incidents that occur will just drop dramatically. When college teams have done that – no more alcohol sales – the number of arrests and people getting kicked out of stadiums has just dropped so dramatically it just makes you laugh," Wann said, as we started to dig into solutions to the problem of poor fan behavior. "So first and foremost, get rid of the alcohol. But they're not going to do that, right? Do you expect that they'll stop selling alcohol at Coors Field? How about Busch Stadium? Miller Park? I doubt it."

So maybe there isn't a solution that the NFL can control. Nevertheless, we still have not determined why fans resort to violence – against family members, themselves, and each other – in the first place. The study published by Card and Dahl draws an inarguably reliable connection between the intensely emotional connection diehard sports fans share with their favorite teams and a lack of self-control. The fan is most susceptible to the latter when an unexpected and negative outcome occurs in the game. Add alcohol to the mix and you are looking at a dangerous combination that can only lead to terrible, terrible things at the home. If the violence sparked by sports fans was limited to a specific league and specific necessary ingredients, maybe people smarter than I am could actually come up with a way to minimize violence and help people help themselves. Unfortunately, it is not that simple. In fact, fan violence represents a complex web of circumstances often unpredictable and, sadly, unavoidable. The one constant seems to be the same thing that makes it possible for diehard sports fans to transcend to that rewarding and beautiful state of euphoria in the best of times: emotional attachment.

"When people are in the middle of such high emotional collective moments they are literally experiencing what we would call trance," anthropologist Gabriel Torres explained. "The mind is in trance-like states very often during sporting events and any sort of standing problem that is a problem of society at large can come to bear during these situations. I might explode during or after a game precisely because whatever dissatisfactions I had in life, especially those dissatisfactions that are collectively held, can lead to riots. This can be collective expressions or they can be individual expressions; people don't just harm others, they harm themselves. You do see alcohol being a big factor often in this sort of thing and of course, that makes us braver." Torres paused for a moment before adding, "You know, sometimes there's no explanation that's obvious. Sometimes it's just cultural phenomena."

That's an astute observation about the human experience. In fact, this whole process of getting to the heart of why we care so much about sports – and within this particular chapter, why some fans resort to violence – has at times led me to wonder if the answer is simply that our passion for our chosen teams is inexplicable. That said, I do think there are a few conclusions that apply to most diehard fans. What I am finding, however, is that some of the most deplorable actions of sports fans are the unfortunate outcome of an unavoidable collision. The formula brings sudden emotional trauma experienced within the sporting world (in other words, a devastating and unexpected loss) together with the emotional baggage carried into the ballpark from the cold, dark world outside.

The idea that fans turn to sports as an escape from reality is a commonly held perception. Even if you have no need to take a break from life's responsibilities – and I would like to think that I'm a reasonably well-adjusted individual living a generally happy and fulfilling life – for those few hours when you're etching away at your score-card or high-fiving with strangers, it is indeed a break. Truth be told, it is easy for even the most balanced individuals to allow themselves to wash away in the tidal wave of excitement when the ball bounces the right way and their team comes out on top. At the end of the game, they return to reality with renewed vigor to tackle the challenges that life throws at us all. On the other hand, the damaged and broken spirits among us also return to real life. After all, the fantasy must end sometime. For these people, a brief respite from their personal hell does not stop the fire from smoldering. Now imagine for a moment when the action in the fantasy world of sports also turns sour – this vacation from reality offers no reprieve at all. The reaction is unpredictable; humans are going to do as humans tend to do in trying times. Some rise above and others, sadly, do not. In other words, as I study the topic and ask the question of why fans choose violence, I find it easier to isolate these incidents as examples of what happens and how we react when the real world rushes back in. When the pleasing fantasy world of sports fandom comes to an abrupt end.

"Correlations are not necessarily causation," Torres said. "I don't think anyone can seriously sustain an argument that sports increases violence in society. That could be a circular argument because violence in society could be the reason why sports are so popular. If you mourn the loss of a team, sometimes it lasts days and you're thinking, 'How come they couldn't win that game?' And as a child who didn't have that fantasy that we could go and replay it? It lingers with people and it's a great cause of stress."

The beauty of anthropology, the study of humans past and present, is that the field offers much broader perspectives on inherent human traits and motives. The external effects that fuel a casual fan's evolution toward becoming a diehard and the reasons why some people handle on-field disappointment in all the wrong ways are as complicated and numerous as the individuals themselves. The extent of our engagement, and how much self-control and perspective we are able to maintain in the best and worst of times vary considerably depending on the person. This is due, in part, to factors seeping in from the outside world. Antagonizing forces beyond the sports arena are often at play when an NFL fan endures the emotional blow of an upsetting and unexpected loss and determines to punish his family for the surprising outcome. There are no absolutes within human relationships, but relationships in good standing tend to produce fewer instances of physical violence. In contrast, the years of police reports Card and Dahl analyzed and categorized likely featured more than a few relationships on the brink of collapse prior to the point when the victimizer crossed the line.

The same holds true for the various Soccer Wars that triggered riots in Latin America and sparked Croatian Independence – symbolically, at least. The game itself did not, and could not, set off the fan violence that marred these matches. Rather, it was what the game represented. For example, nationalist pride amid a volatile political environment in the instance of the Balkan Soccer Wars. Unique political, economic or familial influences infuse each scenario, but the common thread is a compounding effect and reaction that comes with blending an explosive, emotional moment on the playing field with pre-existing tensions between groups. To that end, it's important to dig a few layers deeper and understand the broader context of the human lives involved while grasping for answers about why fans become violent.

In the developed world, I find it curious that fans of opposing teams occasionally find it so difficult to get along with one another. For example, in the U.S., we are fortunate to soak in sporting events without frequent interference from political, economic, cultural or religious forces. Once the verbal barbs and witty quips subside, is it that difficult to enjoy each other's company and recognize that while some people may root for different uniforms, diehard fans are all madly in love with the same game? As a fan of my respective teams, I root passionately against their fiercest rivals. I will admit that I scoff at rival fans sitting within earshot who fail to recognize their proper place in the food chain of fandom when supporting the visiting team. In other words, cheer for your team quietly and politely – you are a guest in our home. At the same time, I can appreciate the fan experience and diehard passion that may exist in other parts of the country and yes, even among my team's rivals. Running into fans of other teams often leads me back to people much like myself who just happen to have chosen the wrong team. That's me, but fans come in all shapes, sizes, and ideologies when it comes to acceptable decorum regarding interactions between rival fans.

"You have highly identified fans – the ones who are really diehards – but you also have dysfunctional fans. These [dysfunctional fans] are fans that thrive on complaining and being confrontational – the dude that sits in the very last row of the top deck and sits there for nine innings cussing at the home plate umpire. When you couple a highly identified and a dysfunctional fan [as one fan], you've got a fan who is probably going to be looking to blow off. They come into the stadium wired for violent actions – that's at the individual psychological level," said Wann when our discussion settled on violent behavior between fans. "At the sociological level, the fact that you're sitting in a group of 25, 35, 45,000 people, it just gives us this feeling of being anonymous and we can sort of do whatever we want and get away with it because no one is going to know it was us."

Living in the San Francisco Bay Area, I have the opportunity to bear witness to one of the longest-running and most spirited rivalries in the history of competitive sports. That I am a fan of neither the local San Francisco Giants nor the Los Angeles Dodgers does not lessen the enjoyment I get from watching two bitter rivals face one another between the white lines. For most rivalries to reach their fever pitch, both parties must be performing well. However, the competitive fire between the Giants and Dodgers stands the test of time regardless of their rankings in the standings and dates back to the days when they would battle at the fabled Polo Grounds and Ebbetts Field in New York. I can only imagine what it was like to be part of the excitement when these two squads came together on the diamond some 60 years ago on the other side of the country, back before fans wore ridiculous panda hats and the Manny Ramirez trade to L.A. birthed the unfortunate moniker of "Mannywood." Fans of the cross-town (and now, cross-state) rivals have bumped heads consistently since that first encounter in 1890 (a 7-3 victory by what were then the Brooklyn Bridegrooms). Off-the-field incidents surrounding the Giants-Dodgers rivalry, however, have gained greater notoriety in recent times and often occur with limited provocation. In fact, during instances of extreme violence at either ballpark in the past few years, the perpetrators are often not even fans at all. Rather, they're dangerous people simply looking for trouble and using the convenient excuse of a fierce sports rivalry to start it. That said, the fact remains that fans of opposing teams do fight one another on occasion. When they do, the spark can be as simple as the logo on their hats as psychology professor Sommers, who has researched such things, explained.

"The flipside of affiliating with certain people and having social affiliations is that it usually means you're drawing distinctions between yourself and other people," he said. "You should be able to respect diehards of any sport, but this [fighting between fans] is a bastardization of what sports is supposed to be about. When you draw lines around an in-group and for a variety of facts, competition for scarce resources tends to lead to prejudice and inter-group conflict and that's what you're doing in the world of sports. Certainly, when you talk about adding alcohol and stuff to the mix along those lines then that's going to cause serious problems."

Fans misbehave and sometimes, the bad behavior spins out of control. Attend live games and you will undoubtedly witness both the best of humankind and some of the worst. How we carry on as we cheer our teams in good times and bad is a matter of choice and, perhaps surprisingly, most fans make good decisions.

"Every person I know that studies sports fandom at the psychological and sociological level agrees with me that they're amazed that there aren't more crazy things happening given the level at which fans care about their teams," Wann said. He acknowledges that for all the hand-wringing about protecting fans from themselves, the vast majority of the millions filing through the turnstiles each season across the sports world are typically there to watch the game peacefully. "Given the levels at which our society has become increasingly uncivil and given the level at which people in a crowd will do things they wouldn't otherwise do, fans are amazingly well behaved," he said. "One bad action is a bad action, but it's amazing that so many of them are doing the right thing."

9
LOYALTY

Ghostly shadows peek around every corner of the concrete oval as we move slowly through the empty corridors of the Scottrade Center in St. Louis. Between October and June, the arena is bustling with noise and energy. That's when the city's hockey club, the Blues, don the blue note logo across their chest and skate at breakneck pace in the arena they call home. Our pace, as we continue our journey toward the top deck of the arena, moves along a few steps slower. Dressed in baseball caps and the ultra-casual apparel more appropriate for St. Louis Cardinals baseball in July than Blues hockey, we're out of place here. Around every turn, images of heavily padded gladiators remind us that we are strangers in a strange land. Our shoes squeak along the glistening corridor as light bounces off the polished floor from an occasional window to the outside world along our way. Hints of the future lurk around every corner: the food vendors with metal gates padlocked to countertops and shadowy gift shops with images of toothless warriors visible just beyond barred doors. We are here for baseball, however, because we've been told that a small collection of hardball artifacts resides somewhere within these walls. It is here that the lasting memory of the moribund St. Louis Browns baseball franchise maintains its faint pulse. These hollow arteries nestled in the heart of downtown St. Louis offer an education to arena wanderers about a team that, more than 60 years ago, spurned the city of St. Louis for greener pastures in Baltimore.

Yes, the city of St. Louis, the Gateway to the West, once fielded two professional ball clubs. Our present-day perspective is shaped by a progressive era of advanced metrics, massive television network deals, and quaint downtown ballparks so numerous that they're starting to become just as cookie-cutter as the parks they replaced. Because of this, it is easy to forget about the team that shared a city and its history with the most successful franchise in the National League. The Browns called Sportsman's Park home from 1902 until 1953, and even its most ardent supporters can admit that it is a history noted for failure more than anything else. In fact, after spending a little time with old-time Browns fans and their descendants, I was left with the impression that they revel in that loss-filled history. The team placed in the basement 14 times across 52 seasons in the Show Me State and managed to creep up to seventh place (second-to-last) on 12 other occasions. If you're keeping score at home, the Browns placed seventh or eighth in an eight-team league across exactly 50 percent of their existence. While the Chicago Cubs continue to chase the dream of World Series glory, now reaching more than 100 years, the team has at least managed a handful of close calls and more than enough winning seasons to keep hope alive for the fans who continue to pour into Wrigley Field each year. The Browns, on the other hand, did not often provide their fans with an on-field product that instilled a sense of confidence that, "this is the year!"

The crowning achievement of the Browns' beleaguered existence is a loss to its crosstown rivals in the 1944 World Series. That's right: even its limited success involves losing to some extent. That defeat would prove to be the final triumph for a team that would ultimately leave town a decade later and evolve into the Baltimore Orioles of today. Sadly, the Orioles do not pay much attention to their legacy in the Midwest. No, to find relics of a bygone era, it pays to be a hockey fan.

High above the rink at Scottrade Center rests a tall display case featuring a few rows of memorabilia associated with Browns history. A collection of hats marked with the Browns logo – and one peculiar little item featuring an elf, which for reasons I can't even begin to explain served as the team's mascot – sits next to black-and-white images of players set against the backdrop of pill box Sportsman's Park. A couple of game-used bats rest against the back wall of the shrine. In the foreground, a handful of baseball cards representing the team's roster through the years spills out across the glass shelving and features sketches of ballplayers rather than photos, as those old Bowman and Topps trading cards often did back in the '40s and '50s. Among the highlights of this miniature memorial is a worn baseball signed by the incomparable Leroy "Satchel" Paige that rests on a shelf of its own next to a card bearing the player's likeness. The former Negro League legend played three years for the Browns beginning at age 44 and concluding his time in St. Louis with respectable numbers (at his advanced age), including 18 of his 28 Major League victories. Surrounding the Paige icon are a couple additional knickknacks and pennants, but little else remains to serve as a reminder of this mediocre band of ballplayers that once called the corner of Dodier Boulevard and North Grand Street home.

At this stage of our exploration of the ruins of Brownie baseball, Bill Rogers, the President of the St. Louis Browns Historical Society and our host for this tour, noticed that a pennant had come unglued from the back wall of the case. Unlocking the cabinet, Rogers crept inside carefully and affixed the keepsake back onto the wall with a few delicate taps. That no one, aside from offseason stadium workers, would see it until the fall makes no difference to the man who continues to carry the mantel for his favorite team, a team that abandoned his city more than 60 years ago. Rogers remains vigilant in his mission to preserve the memory of Browns baseball more than a half-century since he last stepped foot in long-since demolished Sportsman's Park. Even if that heavy responsibility is limited to tending to items in a small cabinet tucked away in the offseason darkness of a cavernous hockey arena.

"My wife debates it with me: 'Why do you do this? Why do you work so hard? People don't even know the Browns.' Wait, hold on – time out," Rogers told me, as he shared the all too familiar construct of a conversation I have had many times with people who can't understand why grown men follow a children's game with such fervor. "I'm not a real history buff, but I do believe in preserving history. I throw the Browns in that category. We need to remember the Browns and that history. And why?" He paused to consider the original question again. "Maybe it's just a quirk of mine, wanting to preserve this."

Rogers takes great pride in the work he has done as President and Chief Operating Officer of the St. Louis Browns Historical Society. He is the caretaker of a long-dead franchise with its history frozen in time forever. He recounted the story of one longtime member of the organization's fan club who included with an annual donation a special request to have his well-worn membership card, acquired in 1985, replaced. "I'm thinking here's a guy that has got that card that he's held onto it now for 30-plus years and he's proud of it and he wants it replaced," he said, with a hint of pride himself. For Rogers, the small things matter most. And he is a proud man, happily tending to the minutiae like pennants peeling off the back wall of a modest exhibit or a member requesting a new identification card proclaiming their affiliation with the Brownie

Brigade. "We're getting ready to do just that. Here's somebody that treasures that memory."

After retiring from a successful career in sales and
management, Rogers, at age 75, has made the preser-
vation of St. Louis' brief history as a two-team city his
second career. He has manned the controls since 2008 and
ushered in an era of lively activity even as the roster of
living Browns alumni dwindles with each passing year. At
the time of this writing, 22 Browns players remain from
a more than 50-year existence as part of Major League
Baseball's junior circuit – the American League. Annually,
Rogers and his team work hard to bring together whatever
living players are still mobile enough to travel to a St. Louis
banquet hall for a reunion. The annual attraction continues to draw more and more attention each year from St.
Louisans and old-time Browns fans even as its celebrity
attendance shrinks as time passes by and people pass on.

Rogers is also part of a dissolving tribe himself: the
faithful disciples of Browns baseball that at one time
helped make Sportsman's Park a great place to spend an
afternoon. Don't tell surviving Browns fans that flagging
attendance figures ultimately led to the team's evacuation
from America's Heartland. As far as tens of thousands of
fans that continue to keep in touch with Rogers and his
contemporaries through the Historical Society are con-
cerned, baseball in St. Louis was the hottest ticket in town.
Looking back, Rogers estimates taking in somewhere
between 15 and 20 games at the old ball yard. The memories are starting to fade for Rogers, but he figured that his
first Browns experience came as World War II ended in
the mid-1940s while the final visit occurred as the team
left town in 1953. Sadly, he just missed the Browns surprise run at the 1944 World Championship, in which they
ceded to the neighboring – and historically more successful – St. Louis Cardinals in the first and only all-St. Louis

World Series. What he does remember vividly, however, is fitting for a fan of a sad sack team like the Browns: a memory about the success of another team altogether.

History is a funny thing. Major League Baseball, the preeminent preservationist of its own rich and lengthy history, reports no single game where Yankees legend Joe DiMaggio hit three home runs in a single contest against the lowly Browns. That's not to say that the Yankee Clipper didn't put on a fireworks show at Sportsman's Park. In fact, in no less than three occasions in 1948 and 1949 – the formative years of Rogers' Browns fandom – DiMaggio rattled Brownie pitchers for two four-baggers, which is a powerful showing in its own right. Yet Rogers holds the line firmly. His lasting memory of attending Browns games at the mid-century mark is of three blasts by one of the game's greatest sluggers. Adding a mythical quality to the story, he described how each mighty blast left the park faster than the one before, and how the final shot climbed halfway up the scoreboard. Who am I to contradict the man's fondest memories with facts?

You read that right: the memories that shaped Rogers' fandom revolved around the New York Yankees using and abusing his team. Such is life as a diehard fan of the St. Louis Browns. When life gives you lemons, make lemonade. A source of pride for Rogers is the Browns' role in bringing legends of the game like DiMaggio (the lemonade) to St. Louis. During this period in American history, most Midwestern fans would never have other-wise caught a glimpse of the players that helped make baseball America's National Pastime. The Browns offered these little sparks of excitement amid the endless losing seasons (the lemons).

"The Browns were responsible for bringing star ball-players to St. Louis like Babe Ruth, Ted Williams, Lou Gehrig and the whole list of players over the years of big time [players]," he said. "If the Browns were not here, the St. Louis fans would have never seen any of those ballplayers. For instance, the people in New Orleans, do they ever see these ballplayers? Back then, no, they missed all those great stars."

Of course, back in the early 1900s through the era immediately following World War II, most of the game's household names – DiMaggio, Ruth, Gehrig, Berra, Mantle, and so many others – wore pinstripes. Money and influence, so prevalent in the game today, had its place in the game even during a period widely referred to as baseball's Golden Age. Certainly, it was the best of times for fans living in St. Louis. Sportsman's Park would be teeming with activity at three o'clock in the afternoon any day of the week while hosting either the Cardinals or those lovable losers in brown and orange, the Browns. The Browns stumbled into a mini-run of success beginning in 1941, culminating in a World Series appearance in 1944. That the Browns' success coincided with a period during which the best players in pro ball suited up in military fatigues rather than their team's colors did the team's legacy no favors. Here was a team, the laughingstock of professional baseball, rising to prominence while the legends of the game lost the best years of their playing careers serving overseas. Great players – and I mean "face of the game" great – like DiMaggio, Williams, Hank Greenberg, and others served as many as four years during wartime. On the other hand, the Browns relinquished only Daffy Dean and a handful of no-names to the call of war. The boys that remained on the playing field during those star-starved war years snuck to the top of the American League standings and overcame baseball's vulnerable, decimated giants.

"Everybody scoffs at the 1944 pennant," Emmett McAuliffe, a St. Louis-based lawyer, and longtime board member of the Browns Historical Society explained. "They said, 'Everyone was gone for the war,' and I say no, that's when everything was equalized. You had this frost that came over and killed the crop. Who won was based on ingenuity and spirit at that point. The influence of cash was dampened in '44 and that's when the Browns saw their opportunity." McAuliffe shared with me the story of how the Browns ascended from the bottom of the barrel to the top of the heap by getting creative with their roster. While the war raged on overseas and Americans came together to support the troops in a number of ways domestically, the Browns found ways to help themselves and put together a winner in an unorthodox fashion. In one such instance, according to McAuliffe, the team reached an agreement with a pitcher working in a munitions plant in Toledo, Ohio. Their unique arrangement called for this man, already quite busy with his current job but possessing an uncanny knack for throwing baseballs, to toe the rubber anytime the team hit the road in Detroit or Cleveland. That turned out to be quite a few games in an eight-team league.

"They had people on 24-hour recall and shuttled them in and out all the time. [The Browns] had rookies that just sat on the bench and never played because they were just filling a spot for the guy who was working at the munitions plant and could only play on the weekends," he continued. "The Browns really wanted to win that year; they felt that this was their opportunity so they manipulated the levers harder than everybody else. They just tried harder."

There's a degree of romance in that, isn't there? Today it's difficult to escape clichés and platitudes in sports, and it's the reason why diehard fans are less than thrilled to listen to national broadcasts of their favorite team's games. National announcers like Joe Buck and Tim McCarver get a bad rap for their hackneyed and overly vague commentary, often exclaiming that this team "wants to win" or that team "wanted it more." That isn't a knock on Buck or McCarver, as I have grown to appreciate their work – perhaps more than most. However, to hear McAuliffe describe it, you can almost imagine yourself stepping back in time to the spring of '44. You can close your eyes and picture the snow drifts thawing across greater St. Louis as Browns management huddled together to brainstorm fresh ideas for how to take a 72-80 franchise to the top of the pile the following summer. The Yankees, even without some of their best players, somehow outclassed the league on their way to 98 wins and a four-games-to-one World Series win over the Cardinals. The Cardinals' success served as a harbinger of the Browns' future in a way, as it seems difficult to imagine a two-team city keeping a perennial loser in town with a proven winner playing in the same ballpark. Yes, it would take a special kind of ingenuity to upend the defending champs in 1944. *Say, how about that kid up in Toledo? Hell of an arm,* they might have said. *He's working the munitions plant, but I'll bet we can pitch him every Sunday afternoon. He wants to win and by golly, I think we've got the team and the smarts to do it!*

Yes, a decidedly romantic aura draws people back to Brownie baseball year after year. Even though the team hasn't played a game for 60 years, and even though they left in the middle of St. Louis' heyday as a premier civic center. In terms of why people maintain strong connections to the Browns, McAuliffe pointed out that while many other professional teams have come and gone over the years, most have managed to keep their legacy alive through consistency. For example, when the Dodgers left Brooklyn for Los Angeles, the team traded only their mailing address. What it means to be a Dodger fan and wear "Dodger Blue" around town endures today, though perhaps with a few "only in Hollywood" tweaks. For example,

I don't think too many women were strolling through the streets of Brooklyn in designer Dodgers dresses or six-inch Dodgers heels. Marketers have indeed latched onto Hollywood culture to introduce new ways of bringing that classic blue and white to the forefront of fashion in this image-conscious region. In any case, whether in Brooklyn or Los Angeles, Dodger baseball maintained a degree of consistency despite a tumultuous relocation that alienated an entire borough of New York City. Similarly, the Dodgers' partners in crime – the other team that fled New York for California riches – the New York Giants held on tight to their name, colors, and players. Willie Mays patrolled the outfield at the Polo Grounds and, today, gingerly maneuvers along the corridors of AT&T Park to watch his beloved San Francisco Giants go to work in one of the sport's present-day architectural wonders. The Giants are the Giants, in New York or San Francisco. Another East Coast transplant, the Oakland Athletics, did change colors (trading blue and white for green and gold) from their early days as Philadelphia's American League team. However, the name remains the same. The A's are the A's wherever they are and wherever they go. Even during a miserable 12-year mistake in Kansas City. The Browns? The Browns are dead, buried in the fall of 1953. Survived by a small collection of frustrated teenagers that would never understand why their team abandoned them.

McAuliffe, a man that had never seen a Browns game in person, fell in love with the Browns due to the mystery surrounding this alternate universe of colors, uniforms and players that contrasted nicely against the current franchise that calls St. Louis home. In an interview, he referenced the concept of "Earth One" and "Earth Two," popularized in the early 1960s – formative years for McAuliffe – by the DC Comics franchise. On Earth One, you have the Cardinals that St. Louisans today know and love. The

Browns then are the Cardinals of Earth Two. They donned the same S-T-L logo hat, but in shades of brown and orange. The team shared the same address at Sportsman's Park, but alternated home dates. The players were different, but uniquely juxtaposed against one another. This was Earth Two in real life. And if you happen to be a fan of baseball history living in St. Louis with a soft spot for underdogs, the Browns represented the runt in the litter. The Baltimore Orioles chose to celebrate their state bird rather than establishing continuity with the relocating Browns franchise and that only adds layers of allure and mystique to being a Browns fan today. For what it's worth, I think Baltimore Browns has a nice ring to it. We will never know if others might have felt the same way. "I call us America's defunct team," McAuliffe said, referencing a slightly bastardized version of the "America's Team" moniker used to describe both the Dallas Cowboys of the NFL since the late-1970s and Atlanta Braves in the early 1980s, respectively.

"If you're one of those people that thinks there's something slightly missing about today's baseball and you can't put your finger on it, and you want to look back into what might be called the Golden Age, the Browns offer a handy way to do it," he continued. "If you say Browns, you're saying 'Golden Age.' [This era came] before interleague trades, before the DH, before a lot of the changes in baseball and the big money. It's back in the days when people had to take off work to go to the ballpark at three o'clock. If you want to be taken back, you can do it without distraction by being a Browns fan. You can go back and research Philadelphia Athletics history, but at some point, you're going to be pulled forward. Whereas with the Browns, you can just simply go back and enjoy those days."

For Browns fans living in the modern world, loyalty to this defunct franchise is tied equally to fantasy and nostalgia. As McAuliffe put it, serving as a board member for the last bastion of Browns baseball fulfills the fantasy of every sandlot kid with a pack of baseball cards and a dream. "It's like owning your own major league franchise," he said. "It's fantasy baseball in the sense that you own your own team, it's just that they don't play any games anymore." On the other side of the equation – the complicated components that bring people like McAuliffe and Rogers together – is loyalty. The thread that ties every last diehard baseball fan to one another and to the nine men simultaneously at work and play on beautifully cut grass and a dusty clay infield. I am an Oakland Athletics fan conditioned to endure season after season of roster turnover. Out here, fans subscribe to the mantra of rooting for the name on the front of the jersey, not the name on the back. Let's face it – in Oakland, wholesale changes occur every offseason to the names on the back. Coming from that perspective, I was struck by Rogers' persistence in celebrating every last Brownie to ever don the earth tones of his local ball club. He's a diehard, through and through, of St. Louis' forgotten franchise. Now, nearly a lifetime past its expiration date, he is the ultimate cheerleader for any player who trotted out onto the field to go to battle for the St. Louis Browns.

"The ironic thing is that players like Bud Thomas and Roy Sievers – the ones who come back regularly, at the time [of their signing with the Browns] they probably thought, 'Oh man, the Browns. I got signed to one of the worst franchises, what a bummer.' But now, they're more famous because they're Browns," McAuliffe said. "Bud Thomas had a cup of coffee – he played pretty well for two months, but never got back again. You can find Cardinal players in their 80s that played for two months, and nobody knows their name and nobody invites them to banquets because they're not Lou Brock or Curt Flood. So ironically, being a Brown becomes their claim to fame." In other words, they're famous because fans like Rogers and McAuliffe have dedicated extraordinary efforts to keeping their memory alive. In Browns Country, just making it to the big leagues enshrines you forever in the Hall of Fame of Browns Legends.

"[My wife] says I'm stuck in the 1950s," Rogers said as we wrapped up our conversation. "Well, I may be. I don't mind being stuck in the '50s. I had fun back then and I'm having fun with it now."

For the St. Louis Browns, the 1950s live on in the cavernous corridors of the city's Scottrade Center. Hockey fans will walk past, beer in hand, wondering what to make of that little Brown elf staring back at them from beyond the glass case. They won't appreciate the pennants, pinned painstakingly to the wall by a devoted, faithful caretaker. As they tuck back into the arena and roar with approval the next time the Blues light the lamp on the ice below, they will quickly forget their momentary glance back in time at ghosts of St. Louis' past. However, as much as the display is for them – for the continued education of St. Louisans about their two-team baseball past – it isn't for them. These archives are for the Brownie Brigade. They exist for people like Emmett McAuliffe, who never saw a Browns game, but longs for a time when the game was a game and not the business of the game. This faint pulse, the heartbeat of Browns baseball, is also for the no-name players who make an annual pilgrimage back to St. Louis. Back home. A place where they can hold court and share tales of a short life in the big leagues with the world's sorriest – and arguably, the most beloved – sports franchise. Most of all, the 21st century Browns are for Bill Rogers and the thousands of longtime Browns fans just like him. The young boys and girls who snuck into Sportsman's Park on weekday afternoons after school and watched in awe as the game's legends had their way with the hometown Browns. The young boys and girls who are now older men and women who still love the Browns just as they did 60 years earlier. Back then, and now, it matters little that their team seldom won. The St. Louis Browns represented much more than just a team to root for and ride the highs and lows of competitive sports. No, the Browns constituted admission into a secret society. A corporation comprised of impressionable youth that found their way to the yard some weekday afternoon and gained their first exposure to the beautiful game of baseball at Sportsman's Park.

"I keep coming back to the magic of the diamond. They laid this thing out 150 years ago and it's still producing close plays at first base and RBI (runs batted in) situations with two outs and grand slam home runs and everything about it sounds right," McAuliffe said. "There's something eternal about what is wrought on that diamond, and it matters. Something eternal that just seems to have significance greater than it might be. We can always tie it up in the bottom of the ninth and go on to play another inning."

Amen.

10
FANS AND FAMILY LIFE

My fondest memories as a diehard sports fan revolve around the times I have attended games with the people in my life that I cherish most. Since her birth in 2011, I have taken my daughter to a handful of Oakland Athletics games each season. Certainly, it should not surprise you that toddlers have short attention spans. She does not always fixate on the field of play like her daddy. No, my little girl has a list of demands and she is not shy about submitting it regardless of the inning or in-game situation. These may include wandering the concourse aimlessly for a few innings, getting candy and ice cream, or taking in any number of distractions that define the modern day ballgame experience – the Stomper Fun Zone at our home ballpark, for example. Then, on the other hand, there are glimmers of budding fandom that spring to life as clapping and dancing, singing and squealing, and unfiltered enthusiasm for the game her proud daddy loves so much. I am mindful not to push her too far toward my interests. At the same time, I'm hopefully optimistic that as she grows older, my little girl will always enjoy spending an afternoon at the ballpark with her Dad no matter where her path may lead. Hearing her yell, "Let's go Oakin" (toddler-speak for "Oakland") will never grow old. Ever.

Her mother, my wife, is less enthusiastic. She is supportive of her husband's curious interest in watching grown men throw balls at one another, but let's just say that I have yet to catch her sorting through her secret stash of baseball cards. Even still, I will never forget the excitement beaming from her face the first time we watched fireworks together while sitting on the outfield grass inside the O.co Coliseum. Her tiny frame jumping with every booming explosion with shrieks of, "Wow!" accompanying each as the sky above filled with flashing lights. "It looks like they're coming at us!" she screamed. The night, which featured an edge-of-your-seat (for me, at least) pitcher's duel for the first three hours, closed with the explosions I had hoped the offense might have provided earlier. Pro tip: offense tends to make the game experience better for casual fans and people who might prefer to be elsewhere.

Diehard fans do not always come pre-packaged with an entourage of sports-loving family members. Some of us live with people who will likely never understand our endless fascination with an activity that outsiders see as wholly unproductive. In other words, watching strangers compete against one another for hours does not keep the laundry moving. Getting to the game well before the first pitch in order to tailgate properly does not keep the kitchen cabinets stocked with fresh groceries. Fans and non-fans disagree about where sport falls on the priority list. That's okay, and it's quite healthy. During my own marriage to a non-fan – I still hold out hope that one day, she will slide down that slippery slope to fandom – we have learned to compartmentalize our personal pursuits and interests into their respective buckets. We do this in order to maximize the time we're able to spend together enjoying shared passions. This exercise in compromise and submission to the greater good of our relationship works for us. I have learned to keep my diehard fandom at a pitch just shy of the point where it might, oh I don't know, shatter all the windows in our home with its searing melody. I coast along at that level resting just a rung or two below the stage where we might find my own devotion to team bubbling over into a frothy mess of blubbering emotions and misdirected passion that bypasses my wife for the welcoming embrace of baseball. I'm sorry, I blacked out for a moment. Where was I? You can see how that might get weird quickly if left unchecked.

I joke, but the beauty and the curse of competitive sports is that it's easy to get caught up in the machine. This is especially true if the fan's experience features those tension-filled, action-packed payoffs that can happen anytime and anywhere. Being a fan brings the richest emotional payoff, but at its worst, it's just as easy to allow the most important things in your life to wash out to sea. That search for euphoria addressed throughout these pages, and the community building that lifts us up to the borderline religious experiences we seek, can just as easily tear us down without adequate self-awareness. Fans love the thrill of competition, and sometimes, the pull of sports away from loved ones happens so discreetly that it is hard to know when it is time to course-correct. Love of sport and love of partner differ greatly in the experience that each delivers, but those differences may not seem so obvious to the spurned partner left alone due to the pull of sports.

"I've had women describe men who are into their sports as [feeling] like there's another woman in the relationship or 'he's up to something,'" New York City-based psychotherapist Jonathan Alpert explained. We spoke about recurring themes in his work helping couples navigate difficulties in their relationships caused by sports obsession. "I think the impact can be as huge as if there was someone else in the relationship."

Alpert helps couples to overcome relationship issues, and sports fanaticism has played the antagonist on more than one occasion. As he walked me through different scenarios featuring sports-obsessed husbands or wives and their frustrated partners, I initially had a hard time with the idea that overzealous fandom could be as damaging as infidelity or the notion of the latter – meaning, growing distrust and doubt that a partner is remaining faithful – could be fueled by otherwise innocent nights at the ballpark. It started to click for me, however, when Alpert started calling out a few of the elements of his own book, *Be Fearless*, in which he offers a guide for people to get past what holds them back in their lives. For most, the insurmountable, invisible wall is one built from its very foundation out of fear and uncertainty. These feelings emerge when one partner lacks confidence that both partners have invested equally in the relationship. For the partner uninterested in sports, perhaps already agitated by a lack of attention or fizzling passion in the union, watching their spouse race out the door for hours of sports consumption can absolutely spark feelings of fear and uncertainty. Where is he going when the car pulls away? Even if only just to the arena, the effect can be just as damaging because a choice is made, unwittingly as it might be. "If there are problems already in the relationship – lack of fulfillment, communications problems, sexual problems, so on and so forth – then this will only make matters worse because the woman or guy will feel like he's choosing sports over her," Alpert said. "So she'll feel less important and that will only create bigger problems. If there are already problems in the relationship, this will only magnify them."

I discussed with Laslocky, the heartbreak expert, the comment Alpert made about sports obsession serving as "the other woman" in a flagging relationship to get her take on the competition for attention between loved ones and loved hobbies. She thought that attachment theory, which describes the relationship dynamics between people (and notably, not a relationship between people and the sports teams they love), could be at play. The attachment we crave between people fragments when a spouse chooses to spend a disproportionate amount of time tending to sports interests. In this scenario, the third person in the relationship is the attachment to a favorite sports team. That attachment runs deep when the team's performance provides fulfillment for the fan. When the team starts going sideways, however, there might be a trickle-down effect in other areas of the fan's life. The rejected partner – the diehard in this scenario – searches for a way to cope with the disappointment much as he might when love goes sour, but the negative feelings can leave the fan feeling detached not only from the game that has let them down, but from the people around them as well.

"When you become attached to somebody, and you're in an intimate relationship with them, your neurons are constructed to reinforce that attachment," she explained. She was also quick to point out that she is not a neurologist and what she would say next revolved around an entirely hypothetical and unsubstantiated scenario – 'just bullsh*tting,' as she put it. "If somebody is deeply attached to a team and to the notion of the future of the team the way you would the future of a relationship and they don't wind up becoming the champions, maybe what's happening is those neurons are having to be reconfigured in the same way much like they would in a relationship with a person."

It doesn't have to be this way, of course. Sports fans can embrace the game and their partner without snubbing one for the other. Because buried deep within the DNA of diehard sports fans is a capacity to love and express passion. The Game draws fans to it for different reasons and we consume the action in different ways. However, the basic reaction exhibited by diehard fans to the drama that unfolds on the playing field each day invokes a similar outpouring of emotion across the spectrum of fans. We cheer and groan, hug and clap, yell and chant – all of it a public demonstration of our ability to be vulnerable, emotional animals. Our existence as vulnerable and emotional animals is also what allows us to love and be loved by other people.

"Devotion and loyalty – these are positive traits. I've tried to explain to the partner or the woman or whoever it might be, look, this isn't the worst thing in the world. This shows that he has the ability to be devoted. He's loyal to an interest of his, and he has the ability to show some passion," Alpert, a Boston Red Sox fan himself, said. "It's just misdirected so the woman or the partner feels left out so I try to get the person to recognize it and see if they can redirect some of that passion towards the partner. I try to get the partner to understand that he's not out there doing drugs or doing illegal things. It's not a bad thing that he's into sports. He just has to learn how to manage the time better and learn how to compromise."

Fans pour heart and soul into their team, and the emotional connection to the experience can run incredibly deep – as if they are, in fact, in a relationship with the experience itself. I refer to sports as "an experience" because I think it's important to make a distinction here between following a team and engulfing yourself in everything that comes with being a sincere, diehard fan. I come back to baseball as my muse because there is already such romance stitched into the fabric of our national pastime. You can walk into an old ballpark like Wrigley Field, and settle into your seat with a scorecard, pencil, and overpriced ballpark food. Aside from the modern music and flashing scoreboard lights, this experience is nearly identical to what you might have found some 50, even 100 years earlier. Within the Friendly Confines of Wrigley, they've even kept the organ finely tuned to deliver modern hits with a little touch of history. I find it hard to not fall madly in love with an experience like that. How then, can something so beautiful and with such a rich tradition of bringing people together at the same time drive so many people apart?

Being a fan and continuing to maintain healthy, functioning relationships with other human beings requires empathy and situational awareness. When fans align with a sports franchise, the evolution to diehard status does not occur overnight – it is a process, much like falling in love. Transcending from level to level of fandom requires nurturing and stoking the flames of that passion. As attentive as we are to our burgeoning sporting interests, we must be just as diligent about tending to our responsibilities at home. In essence, sports split up families only when the diehard fan, losing a grasp on the other areas of import in his or her life, stops paying attention to the bigger picture. That big picture view can become cloudy when he or she fails to recognize that following sports just a tad too closely can isolate the fan from friends and family. In other words, the non-fan partner is not going to understand why attending a playoff game is a God-given right when the preseason agreement had been set for a certain number of games. Not because they want to be unreasonable, but rather, they just don't understand the difference. In many cases, this is because the sports fan hasn't taken the time to explain it to them and involve them in their passion.

"The person feels a sense of privilege or entitlement, like, 'I know we only agreed to one day a week, but they're in the playoffs, so I have to see it.' So they seem to bend the rules a bit; it's almost like they expect to get a pass on things because of the playoffs," Alpert explained. "The non-fan doesn't understand because they're not used to sports, and they don't understand the impact or just how important it is. Really trying to educate the person on what the game is about and if possible, taking them to the game could be helpful."

Alpert mentioned the benefits of indoctrinating a spouse to the live game experience several times when we spoke. Can the nonbeliever be converted? Absolutely. First-hand encounters with the game while sitting alongside their beloved diehard can at least serve to establish some degree of understanding about the appeal of such an endeavor. Witnessing the madness of a bases-clearing triple or celebrating a walk-off winner in the company of thousands of other people jumping for joy are moments that, as Torres established earlier, create a sense of community and camaraderie within the ballpark. Shared with a loved one, they can also serve to strengthen both fan and family bonds alike.

"It's really just a matter of creatively compromising," Alpert said. "Try to explain to her why you have such a passion. Take the time to teach her about the game, and then one of the things that I've seen that really helps is taking her to a live game because even if you're not into sports, going to a live game is exciting." He mentioned the singing of the National Anthem – something easily taken for granted with enough visits to the stadium. The pomp and circumstance at play before the game even begins can be just as thrilling for the non-fan as the action on the field for the diehard. For my wife? It's ice cream – always the ice cream. "Maybe the person can learn to appreciate the culture of the game or the sports event – that seems to help a lot."

When I reflect on my roots as a baseball fan, I often think back to my childhood. I recall fondly a time when the game was so much bigger than myself. My excitement not yet poisoned by exposure to the business side of sports or the sterile new age of measuring game day performance with advanced analytics and newfangled acronyms like WAR, VORP and xFIP. No, I liked batting average, home runs, steals, and runs batted in (I will admit that I do appreciate and accept certain advanced metrics today). So much so, in fact, that when I was not watching or reading about baseball, I was assigning fictitious stats to the rotation of shirts I wore each week to elementary school – yes, my clothing. If I had a good day, my shirt received favorable "game day" stats. If not, well, the formula was not complex. You can probably imagine that the day's shirt selection quickly found its way into a thankless long relief role (or in real-life scenarios that make sense: the back of the closet). In any case, I watched many games with my mother during those years. While we would both cheer hysterically, I'm convinced to this day she still has no idea why ballplayers don't try to get to first base on a foul ball. Or why balks advance runners to the next base. Or really, what a "balk" is in the first place. Nevertheless, she loved it, and she still does, because I did and I do. I think back to a time when the All-Star Game and World Series were special because both served as my only opportunity each season to see players from both the American and National Leagues lock horns. In an era during which the Major League schedule features at least one interleague game each day, it's easy to forget how strange these encounters seemed during the Midsummer Classic or to close out the season with the World Series in October. During those early years of my burgeoning fandom, the only options available to me were to watch the Philadelphia Phillies on PHL 17 or flip to the New York broadcasts to watch the rival Mets and Yankees. Even at that time, I felt nostalgic for times even further back in the annals of history. I loved the game as it existed during my formative years, but the fact that I could do a little reading and uncover a bygone era filled with fascinating intersections connecting sports to current events proved wildly appealing and drew me in like a moth to the flame. I loved flipping over an old baseball card to discover that during World War II, professional athletes – the most talented in the league, mind you – missed years of their prime playing days for military service. My jaw dropped when I learned that a journeyman catcher named Moe Berg doubled as a spy for the Central Intelligence Agency during trips to Japan in the mid-1930s.

I share all of this with you because something Alpert said stuck with me long after we wrapped up our conversation. If we spent 15 minutes talking about the balance of fandom with the responsibilities of family life, we spent twice as long waxing nostalgic about old ballparks and the cultural significance of America's oldest game. Moments in our history on Earth are woven together so tightly with the great game of baseball that the two are indistinguishable from one another. When Jackie Robinson broke the color barrier in Major League Baseball in 1947, the moment transcended the sport and accelerated our progression toward being able to live together peacefully as a human race. More than fifty years later, the New York Mets played host to the Atlanta Braves in a gripping, emotional contest 10 days after the World Trade Center attacks of September 11, 2001. On that night, larger than life ballplayers cried, fans packed the stadium, and a nation paralyzed by fear began to heal. More recently, Dominican-born David "Big Papi" Ortiz, in a moment that would resonate with the entire country wounded again by an act of terror at the 2013 Boston Marathon, proclaimed, "This is our f**king city and nobody is going to dictate our freedom. Stay strong!" Such strong language should have offended, but few complained. Even FCC chairman Julius Genachowski stepped forward on Twitter to support the heartfelt comment made by the Red Sox icon. At that moment, in that city and enveloped within the haunted concourses of that oddly shaped ballpark, it was perfect. Even the staunchest critics of professional sports can appreciate the degree to which sports can help nations heal.

"History plays out on the ball field," Alpert had commented. He's right, and I don't think there's much of an argument to the contrary. "As a kid I was a baseball fanatic. For me, it's nostalgic and it sort of associates me back to when I was a kid. I think for a lot of people that's the case; the game is rooted in rich tradition and it's just part of our culture."

Thinking about this comparison calls to mind another reason we file into the ballpark in droves, and why some choose team over family whether they realize the consequences or not. We believe we are witnessing history reveal itself with each pitch. We hope that we might be fortunate enough to behold something – anything at all – of significance. Either that or we're nostalgic for times when it was just us and our ballgames, coming through in analog. Alpert reminded me that maintaining personal interests is healthy and important. Go to a ballgame and experience history unfolding before your very eyes. However, when this pursuit begins to overshadow our family relationships, that's when all the nostalgia in the world and cultural relevance goes right out of the window and the obsession becomes a problem. In these instances, we've crossed over into a selfish pursuit of the transcendent when those moments are, in fact, meant to be shared.

"A diehard sports fan is someone who has developed a passion around a healthy activity," Alpert said. "There's also a sense of community and the opportunity to make friends, so it's a really good activity. Having said all that, if it goes to the extreme, it's quite the opposite. Moderation is key."

11
SPORTS FANDOM
AND THE BRAIN

The human brain is immensely complicated. In recent times, sports leagues have invested millions into researching the impacts of, well, impact, on our most valuable physical asset. Figuring out a plausible counter-offensive to the hockey stick trajectory of concussions on the playing field has emerged as a priority in recent years as leagues aim to protect their athletes. Major League Baseball tinkered with larger helmets that, while cartoonish in appearance, offered greater protection for batters staring down a tiny white pill careening toward their head at 100 miles per hour. At the time of this writing, that experiment has failed to catch on. The great deterrent of vanity made players awfully aware of how ridiculous they looked. Even catchers, the warriors of baseball with their own excessive body armor sanctioned by the rulebook, remain at the mercy of the unpredictable path of the batted ball and wildly over-swung bat. The league, recognizing that head injuries – and more specifically, brain injuries – differ considerably from the myriad ailments that send players to the 15-day disabled list, created a separate seven-day distinction just for concussion recovery. As a sports fan today, I am hyper aware of the prevalence of concussions because the athletes I watch seem to cycle continually through that seven-day brain time out. As a child, I was only aware of such head injuries because I watched a whole lot of hockey and I watched young men retire from the game in their mid-20s due to repeat head injuries. Perhaps it was naïve, but the rate of concussions seen across all leagues today seemed unfathomable in those days. It is scary to think about how many players continued to risk permanent brain damage simply by floating through their careers without proper diagnosis.

The National Football League, which persistently – and commendably – evolves its armor to improve coverage and the safety of its players, went so far as to change its rules to reduce helmet-to-helmet contact. Such rule changes have caused great consternation, particularly among defensive players. Hard-hitting safeties and linebackers had made a living by de-cleating (that is to say, tackling in the most violent and forceful manner possible in which case the recipient of the blow is sent pirouetting through the air) defenseless wide receivers foolish enough to risk life and limb with every reckless scamper across the middle of the field. Now, we enter an era of indecisive defenders making last-minute course-corrections to change their approach and avoid penalty and, instead, levy awkward and poorly timed hits that are creating completely new types of injuries. The NFL gets points for trying, I suppose.

Major League Baseball similarly nixed home plate collisions between base runners and catchers in the wake of several horrific injuries to catchers after they were trucked on close plays at the plate. Collisions and, by proxy, season-ending injuries to catchers dropped through the floor from one year to the next. Yet even with the players finally protected from the deathblow of a full-grown man bearing down at full speed, that rule has also come under fire. League officials continue to tinker, thanks to a few wonky interpretations and differences of opinion between officials and managers about what constitutes blocking the plate. We may yet see a return to home plate collisions as officials try to determine a better way of re-writing the rulebook to allow for less debate.

And then there's the legacy of brain injury and permanent damage inflicted within the squared circle of the world's most popular non-sport, professional wrestling. For decades, behemoths have crushed each other's skulls with every possible foreign object – though notably, the once-prevalent steel chair is now used sparingly in today's more family-friendly World Wrestling Entertainment programs. Professional wrestling at its best resembles a highly orchestrated and complicated ballet. If you aren't watching closely, you might miss that the guy being thrown around like a rag doll is often the better wrestler. His ability to twist and turn like a falling cat is the reason why the punishing body blows and "finishing moves" that appear so damaging still allow the loser to walk or crawl away when the bell rings. Again, that's pro wrestling at its best. At its worst, the damage is incredibly real. Concussions run rampant in the world of professional wrestling, whether the action is scripted or not. For some, the bell never stops ringing and the combatants live with the trauma inflicted by the countless blows for the rest of their lives, all in the name of entertainment. That's to say nothing of the impact of steroids and other performance-enhancing drugs on the brain. Steroid use is well documented within wrestling circles and only accelerates the athlete's evolution from a Lord of the Ring, impervious to chair shots, to a victim of early onset dementia and Alzheimer's.

That is, of course, a topic for another day. Innumerable brain geniuses with impressive credentials and several years of scholarly training more than I have are in the lab, and on the case. They dig into the inner workings of the human brain and try to find new ways to keep our athletes safe from each other and themselves. They do this because the brain remains our greatest human mystery.

My curiosity, however, rests not with the effects of head injuries on the brain and the human capacity to bounce back. That's a well-worn path that I'll leave to the doctors to resolve and the professional sports leagues to mitigate. Rather, I wondered about the impact that observing sports might have on the makeup of the brain – on having a brain and being a fan, and if one affects the other. The study of sports fans has brought me back, repeatedly, to the irrefutable truth that not everyone is as hopelessly romantic about sports as diehard fans. I have often wondered if there is, in fact, something different about our clan. If there is something unique or strange about me, and people like me, that draws us into an insatiable bloodlust for the drama of sports. Have I had a taste of something so spectacular and addicting, recognized by an indiscriminate cross-section of the world's population, that the fundamental construct of my brain has changed? In short, probably not. And if that's not the answer you were looking for, then you can feel free to move right along to the next chapter. However, there is indeed something phenomenal at work inside the old nut when that sense of euphoria covered in these pages reaches its apex.

"The act of gathering with a community of fans may activate the bonding hormone oxytocin. And in the event of a win, the hypothalamus may release dopamine," Dr. Sandra Bond Chapman, founder and Chief Director of the Center for BrainHealth at The University of Texas at Dallas, explained to me. "Once the brain associates the elated sensations with a team win, it will adapt to seek the rewarding feeling again in the future."

There's that word again: community. Being with other people and celebrating a common interest in a positive outcome releases hormones in the brain, and this is likely true in any pursuit both within sports and far outside of its reach. Our desire to be with other people is why we gather. This is true of political rallies, Disney World's Main Street, and even antique shows where we display, compare, and celebrate our wares with others. And it's also why so few of us choose to live our lives in complete seclusion. The brain instructs us to gather because gathering is good for the brain. And you thought you were in control?

Dr. Leslie-Beth Wish sees something innately human in our capacity to come together and cheer on our favorite sports teams. But then, she would. As a psychologist, licensed clinical social worker, and author of a book, Smart Relationships, she studies why our brain instructs us to do just about anything at all. That covers our capacity to fall in love with people and with sports.

"We human primates want to belong, and part of belonging is the experience of being liked," she said. The heart, it seems, is very much connected to the brain. "The feeling of belonging activates our sense of pleasure and attachment. Being with others with whom we feel close and like arouses the hormone oxytocin, often called the attachment or love hormone. It›s the hormone that prompts mothers to attach to their babies."

While we may not use every particle of that unusual, mystifying and wildly misunderstood sponge that rests between our ears, what little we do use can have a hypnotizing effect on the rest of our self. We've been down this path in earlier chapters – the connection we establish, even if it is a one-way relationship, between ourselves and our favorite sports teams can become frighteningly intense. And yes, perhaps even reaching into that stratosphere of the mother's bond with a child. Within the context of sports fandom and the in-game experience, our brain changes in an instant when we reach that tipping point on the road to euphoria. Why love of sport separates itself from other hobbies and interests (and parenthood), and perhaps why the diehard fan's passion can reach such fervent levels, is that the hormonal changes that sports can have on our brain in "in the moment" scenarios can take us instantly to an entirely different plane of bliss when our team wins. When a positive outcome is uncontested and expected, it still feels good and we still want more. However, when the result of a game is hotly contested and undecided right down to the wire or when a victory is unexpected (I'm reminded of my own unexpectedly pleasant experience outlined in chapter one), something extraordinary happens in our brain. Dopamine flows in like the rush of adrenaline one might experience when jumping out of an airplane or diving into icy water with the Polar Bear Club. Given exposure to such an experience, our brains begin to associate winning with pleasure and we want more and more and more.

"Evidence suggests that dopamine cells respond to a reward primarily when it occurs unpredictably, which is typical with sporting events," Chapman said. "Because our brains want to repeat feelings of pleasure and euphoria, one win may produce a greater desire for the next." As a cognitive neuroscientist and a distinguished academic, Chapman works in close collaboration with scientists around the world to find solutions to some of the most important issues concerning the brain, its health, and potential for advanced performance. In her study, Chapman has sought to uncover new ways to build resilience, help people regain cognitive function when it's lost and retrain the brain to maximize its potential. Luckily, she also happens to be a sports fan with enough personal experience of her own with the highs and lows of fandom where my questions struck enough of a chord to elicit response. Possessing a heightened awareness of the impact of sports fandom on the brain doesn't prevent

Chapman from falling in line with the rest of us living and dying with every moment. "I am an avid sports fan. My love for sports developed in junior high school when I was a cheerleader because our team was one of the best in the city," she said. "I have to care about who wins to watch. I can't just watch; I have to cheer for one team over the other or lose interest."

Like the aging veteran falling painfully short of his first championship and watching the window of opportunity slam shut, we crave that feeling of success constantly. Some fans choose to extract themselves from the pull of fandom when they begin to lose perspective. Fans like Dr. Sam Sommers, the young Tufts professor forced to tamp down his Yankees fervor when the frustrations of living in Boston Red Sox country became too much. Others, however, are consumed by the pursuit of reflective glory and the need for that delightful blend of oxytocin and dopamine rattling around in their brains. Neither scenario counters the fact that our brain computes winning as a positive experience. As competitors ourselves or by basking in the reflective glory of our chosen combatants, goodness gracious, we just can't get enough.

"The brain keeps track of winning and losing, and our brain loves to win; it loves it," Chapman said. Winning, Chapman explained, kicks off the neuro-transmitter we're now beginning to understand here, dopamine, and doing so forever links the winning experience with pleasure. The intensity of that pleasure and the desire for more depends on many of the factors discussed in these pages. These factors include the importance of the game, improbability of the outcome, and the fierceness of the rivalry between the teams on the field. "It's almost the desire to win that triggers this dopamine release, and when you feel it, you really want to keep winning."

According to Chapman, the ability of sports to con-tinually surprise its rabid fan base only intensifies the yearning for that feeling again – euphoria, joy, ecstasy, call it what you want. Wish says these moments when in-game outcomes are uncertain – the edge-of-your-seat, hang-on-every-pitch moments – spark our survival instincts within the brain's amygdala. "You are, of course, not actually in 'combat or run' mode when you are sitting in the stands or watching on television. But our survival needs are so strong that just watching a sport unconsciously makes us imagine we are on the field or court. *Imagining* and *doing* appear almost the same in brain activity."

All major sports with the exception of baseball revolve around tidily restrained parameters: a football field mea-sures 100 yards end-to-end and a period of hockey ticks down from 20 minutes. Professional basketball games are comprised of four 12-minute quarters and, in some cases, the outcome is clear by the end of the third quarter as long as the leading team chooses to take the court in the fourth frame. The clock continues to run in a professional soccer match with the only extension coming in the form of a handful of minutes determined by officials keeping a tally of various injury slowdowns. Baseball, on the other hand, has no end. Down by one run or down by 20, a game is not decided until the umpires call the final out. That may come after two hours or it may come after seven. The only clock is the one that tells us how late we're all staying up when the 18th inning turns into the 19th and the first position player takes the mound to try to survive an inning. For the fans, these moments also provide much-needed comic relief when the crowd begins to run on fumes. The "any-thing can happen" scenario keeps us glued to the action even when our team is down to its final strike behind by a couple runs (true for the diehards, at least). The Oakland Athletics won 20 consecutive games during the summer of

2002, but not before relinquishing an 11-0 lead and forcing a walk-off winner in game number 20. In what many consider the greatest single game comeback in baseball history, the Cleveland Indians beat the Seattle Mariners 15-14 in 11 innings in an August 2001 game during which they had trailed by as many as 12 runs – 12 runs! – as late as the sixth inning. Nothing is impossible on the baseball diamond, but when our team overcomes long odds and near impossibilities, our connection to the game grows stronger. These moments, when we've watched our team steal victory from the jaws of defeat, are the precise ingredients that send our brain into a dopamine-fueled frenzy. These are the times when the seeds of diehard fandom are sowed.

"Evidence suggests that dopamine cells respond to a reward primarily when it occurs unpredictably, which is typical with sporting events," Chapman said. "Because our brains want to repeat feelings of pleasure and euphoria, one win may produce a greater desire for the next."

This isn't the first time in my pursuit of understanding why sports fans care so much about their favorite teams that parallels with addiction have emerged. As diehards, we focus completely on the high – that euphoric condition that overcomes us following an improbable comeback or unexpected performance. We experience sensations like little else in life and our brain begins to associate those good feelings with sports when, beyond our wildest dreams, our team delivers the goods. As such, it adapts to want more. We need to keep our brain's new demands in check, because extreme behavior of any kind can create unsavory outcomes. Drug addicts allow their vice to crawl into every crevice of their lives, and similarly, sports addicts can develop blinders that block out every meaningful aspect of life outside of the game. That's simplifying things a bit, and I'm certainly not implying an "everything in moderation" philosophy regarding illicit drug use. The end game differs significantly. In fact, I would hypothesize that diehard fans have more in common with the developing runner. After months of mastering the discipline required for sticking to a routine, the day comes when an especially satisfying run creates an unexpected response within the body and we're hooked for good. Fueled by the release of endorphins, the brain links this natural high to the act of running. This sensation, perhaps unlike anything experienced in previously sedentary lives, conditions the brain to recognize that running is a good thing. To that end, if a little running is good, more is better. This, to me, feels more aligned with the diehard way of thinking because at its core, being a fan typically drives impacts that are more positive on the human brain than negative.

"Being a diehard fan taps into two great strategies that support having a healthy human brain: following your passion and building social bonds," Chapman said. "Actively engaging with your experience of the game and fellow fans can be a brain booster when you combine your expert knowledge of the game and the team with newly emerging ideas and criticisms."

Sports fandom can turn strangers into lifelong friends, and for social animals, this is an appealing outcome. I know that in my life, the great connector of sports ties all the people I'm closest to, outside of my immediate family, together. Again, if a little is good, more sure seems to be better. So it's through this lens that my wife watched the reach of my fandom extend beyond the teams and sports she had begun to expect me to watch, and into other areas altogether. "I didn't think you liked basketball," she had said as I committed to an Opening Night Golden State Warriors game a few years back. A few years later, this conversation would start again as I tried (successfully!) to explain the importance of locking in playoff tickets to watch this team I began rooting for in 2009 play a game I "didn't like." She wasn't wrong. Basketball had always ranked toward the bottom end of my lists of sports preferences. I didn't dislike the game, as my wife had understood it, but I would much rather sit at a ballpark with a scorecard or put my rooting energy into Philadelphia's football or ice hockey franchises. That changed quickly when I discovered how much joy I could extract from experiencing professional hoops. Basketball didn't spark the flames of fandom until I started spending my evenings at Oracle Arena in Oakland watching Stephen Curry sink three-pointers from 30-plus feet beyond the bucket.

Curry and the Warriors provided one draw, but the other equally powerful pull is that I spent most of my live-game experiences with one specific friend and fellow diehard sports fan. Our conversations from tip-off to confetti (to clarify – postgame confetti can occasionally rain down from the rafters during the postseason) were always riveting and I could feel our friendship grow stronger with each passing quarter of action. This sense of community and friendship, paired with a new appreciation for a sport I quickly began to love, sent the Warriors to a higher level of importance within my sports-viewing life. Our highs during games – fueled by the sweet release of dopamine, I'm learning – were always through the roof. The losses hurt, but I must admit that I have not yet suffered from the same type of devastating emotional damage levied across the street at the O.Co Coliseum while mourning the hardships of the Oakland Athletics. My basketball love affair is a new one, and aside from a few ho-hum seasons in my early rooting days as a Warriors fan, I haven't yet experienced the frustration of a team failing to meet high expectations. Rather, the Warriors' rise to relevance in the Western Conference, which ran parallel to my deepening interest in the team and sport, came with few expectations.

The team provided excitement and when they lost, hey, I didn't really expect them to win a championship anyway – until recently, of course, when the team began to deliver on their championship potential. Meanwhile, my Warriors-loving friend rides the highs and lows of the emotional rollercoaster of every game. I am an evolving diehard. A work in progress. In contrast, my friend bleeds royal blue and golden yellow.

"Some people get happy and some people get really emotional, because dopamine is a highlighter for things like the amygdala, the emotional part of the brain," Chapman said, explaining why a couple of fans might react differently to the same in-game experience. "When you get that set off, you feel even higher. However, when the preferred outcome is not achieved, like in a tough loss to a rival team, less dopamine is released. It can make you really feel lethargic – the feeling permeates everything."

According to Chapman, we have a tendency to feel the losing part of our team's successes and failures far more deeply than the winning. This is especially true for fans that have invested completely. When the shots stop falling and comeback efforts fall a hair short, you go down further than you go up. It's why I felt numb when Detroit shut the Athletics down in the 2013 postseason. Further, it's why my companion for that game couldn't stomach another minute in the ballpark to reflect on another season drawn to an unceremonious close. We went down and we went down hard. In those moments, when our diehard fandom becomes public enemy number one for our hope of a stable mental state, the brain fails to recognize all the happy times sport had provided the six months prior. No, at the moment of utter devastation, we are left only with the wreckage. Nothing short of replaying the game to a different outcome can help us process the terrible end to a terribly good thing – that and the passage of time.

Because as difficult as these low points can be, troubling conclusions to past seasons seem to melt away along with the frost come springtime. The excitement roars back in as we remember the good times with a renewed hopefulness that the next October will bring about a better ending. For the brain, the excitement of Opening Day in any sport can be enough to jump start the flow of dopamine. From day one, we're hooked like a fish on the end of a line, tugged and teased by the Baseball Gods once again.

12

CELEBRATE GOOD TIMES (TOO MUCH)

I have spent a lifetime surrounding myself with losers. Since I was old enough to remember, I have supported and advocated groups of people that continually fail, falling short of even the most attainable and modest of expectations. You don't have to worry about me though. This self-flagellation had minimal effect on me during my formative years because I had known no different. You see, when you identify with Philadelphia sports teams in the mid-1980s, the bar for how much mediocrity you're willing to accept is fairly high.

Sure, the Philadelphia 76ers won the NBA title in 1983, and the Phillies won their first World Series a few months after my birth. How many '80s babies remember those glory years? Instead, I aligned myself with such lovable losers as Von Hayes, Darren Daulton (a big-time loser before he became a big-time winner with the Florida Marlins) and Don Carman. I loved my team because they were my team win or lose (mostly lose). I didn't see any reason why supporting a successful team would have been any different from my experience rooting for the doormats of the National League. That all changed in 2008. Phillies All-Star closer Brad Lidge, successful in each of his 48 save chances that season, buried his best slider behind the swinging bat of Tampa Bay Rays pinch hitter Eric

Hinske for a World Series-clinching swing-and-a-miss on the season's final pitch. Moments later, "Lights Out Lidge" dropped to his knees and screamed, "WE DID IT!" They did it. The Philadelphia Phillies were World Champions, and I was old enough to enjoy, appreciate, and celebrate the only championship I had ever known.

"Now I know what it feels like," I shared in a text message to a friend of mine on that October night. He knew what I meant, as he had been spoiled by no less than five World Series championships in his lifetime as a fan of the New York Yankees. "Pretty great, huh?" was his response. Oh, how I longed to be back on the East Coast on this night. To celebrate in the streets of Philadelphia like only Phillies fans can celebrate. For months, I had bragged to my East Coast friends about how much I loved watching baseball on the West Coast. The games started earlier, and I could listen to Phillies radio broadcasts on my commute home. Who was I kidding? At that moment, while only 3,000 miles away, I may as well have been on the moon. The next morning, I looked on from afar while making a futile attempt to balance productivity with the live webcast of the first and only Phillies World Series parade I would ever see streaming to my computer at the office. The team and the crowd did not disappoint. When All-Star second baseman Chase Utley addressed the masses and uttered the words, "World F**king Champions," the city exploded with a primal roar. I tapped into my sense of responsibility to stay productive. Like a caged animal, I paced around my too-small office. I battled with the temptation to break away to the closest thing I could find out here to a Phillies bar in order to celebrate properly with other transplanted fans. But I resisted. Barricaded in my office, my eyes remained glued to the flood of bodies marching alongside the lengthy caravan of victorious athletes. More than 2 million fans draped in red and white poured onto a four-mile parade route through Center City right into the South Philadelphia home of the city's sporting heroes. That day in 2008 will remain a lasting, positive memory in the hearts and minds of Phillies fans for the rest of their lives. Perhaps some engaged in a bit too much day drinking, but by all accounts, this historically rowdy and boisterous fan base behaved in a manner that would make most of their mothers – and local police – proud.

That had not been the case two days earlier, however, in the immediate afterglow of the team's first title in 28 years and the first championship the city had known in a quarter-century. According to police reports, officers made more than 75 arrests, mostly for acts of vandalism, as fans celebrated along South Broad Street. Marble planters, bus stop shelters, and shop windows suffered the brunt of the alcohol-fueled enthusiasm. When the sun rose at dawn, bonfires, overturned vehicles, and an ocean of glass shards dislodged from storefronts littered the area surrounding Citizens Bank Park. In truth, this destruction hardly registers as a blip on the riot radar if such a thing existed in the archives of celebratory chaos. When contrasted against the post-apocalyptic antics exhibited by celebrants in Detroit following the 1984 World Series win by the Tigers or revelers in Chicago after the Michael Jordan-led Bulls captured the NBA title in 1992, fan behavior in South Philly was downright saintly. Even still, a dark energy lurked beneath the surface of this joyous scene filled with high-fives, hugs, and love. Some people chose to celebrate their team's ultimate success, which creates for most fans a sense of pleasure often unattainable outside of the sporting life, by breaking things. All through the harrowing night and into the next day, these miscreants transformed their hometown streets into something more closely resembling a burned out war zone.

As a diehard baseball fan that has only seen his team make it to the top of the dogpile once in my lifetime, I've never understood this "seek and destroy" mentality. I experienced the Phillies 2008 title at home, quietly, alongside my wife. My wife who, it's worth noting, did a terrific job of providing support while also continuing to read a book with only a passing glance at the mayhem playing out on the television. As if to say, "That's nice. Is it time to watch something else yet?" Would I too be more inclined to set a car on fire if I had a chance to ride the wave of excitement out of the stadium and into the parking lot after a World Series clincher? No, that seems unlikely (everyone take a deep breath). My greatest live sports memory, the Oakland Athletics' shocking victory during a 2012 playoff game, offered many opportunities for bad behavior. I rolled out into the parking lot armed with an adrenaline rush the likes of which I'm not sure I had ever experienced in my lifetime. However, it turns out my reveling behavior is more in-tune with my fellow huggers and high-fivers, rather than the fire-starters and bottle-flingers. So the question remains unanswered: why do fans riot when blessed with the ultimate joy that only the beloved Baseball Gods or other sports deities can offer?

Dr. Robert Silverman, an urban sociologist and professor at the University of Buffalo, has studied these occurrences throughout history. Specifically in cities like Detroit, which has seen its share of riots for reasons far more complex than those presented within the constraints of fandom. While serving as a faculty member within the Sociology Department at Wayne State University, Silverman conducted a great deal of fieldwork on the neighborhoods within the city of Detroit. The mission of his work was to understand and better educate people about the elements that led to substantial decline for more than half a century in the Motor City.

"Certain conditions encourage rioting after games in some places if the economy is bad, if people are frustrated, and they have an opportunity to let their frustrations out after a game during celebrations," Silverman said. "But if you look at college sports, people celebrate after games and students tear down the goal posts and vandalize property around a stadium, and get involved in similar types of behavior where the economic conditions aren't the same [as in cities like Detroit]. You can have other factors like people in their late teens to early-20s having too much alcohol and not being able to celebrate as responsibly as people who might have more experience. You might just have fans that have been waiting years for their team to win and when it finally happens, they get a little bit out of control."

Shortly after World War II, Silverman explained, Detroit's economic prospects took a nosedive. The auto industry moved jobs outside of Detroit's city limits and the migration of the city's populous left people jobless, hopeless, and forced to fight for survival in what would become a dark time for a once-proud urban center. During the 1960s, the people of Detroit faced hardships few endure in a lifetime. Due to its uniquely challenging circumstances, protests in Detroit were just a little bit louder than in other cities, hostilities a little more volatile. Here was a city decimated by a porous job market and mass population migration into suburbia. The future provided few reasons for optimism, few signs that this broken city would ever recover. Detroit's decline coincided with the U.S. civil rights movement, which fanned the flames of discontent in the unsteady 1960s. In 1967, a police raid of an unlicensed after-hours bar sparked a five-day riot, the 12th Street Riot, and led to 43 casualties and more than 1,100 injuries. Just before Opening Day of the 1968 Major League Baseball season, Dr. Martin Luther King's assassination further fractured race relations in a city that could not withstand much more instability, heartache, and despair. But then, the Detroit Tigers won the 1968 World Series. As the city braced for chaos, change was in the air. As 54,692 fans crowded into Busch Stadium some 500 miles away, the entire city of Detroit held its breath. Mickey Lolich coaxed Cardinals batter Tim McCarver to pop out into the glove of Bill Freehan for the final out of the World Series. And, at that moment, normalcy returned to the aching city of Detroit. The riots, for a short time at least, were over. *Detroit Free Press* senior baseball writer Joe Falls put it this way in his October 11 column, which ran the day after the Tigers won the series: "My town, as you know, had the worst riot in our nation's history in the summer of 1967, and it left scars which may never fully heal ... And so, as 1968 dawned and we all started thinking ahead to the hot summer nights in Detroit, the mood of our city was taut. It was apprehensive ... But then something started happening in the middle of 1968. You could pull up to a light at the corner of Clairmount and 12th, which was the hub of last year's riot, and the guy in the next car would have his radio turned up: ' ... McLain looks in for the sign, he's set -- here's the pitch' ... It was a year when an entire community, an entire city, was caught up in a wild, wonderful frenzy." Baseball had healed a grieving city and a beaten-down community found its smile again.

Flash forward 16 years and Detroit was once again a city in decline with no answers for its woes. At the same time, it was, again, a championship-starved city. During the previous decade and a half, the Tigers lost as many as 102 games and, despite several winning seasons and a few close calls, never attained the level of success of that inspired 1968 team. That year, 1984, baseball in Detroit would offer something different. The Tigers jumped out of the gate at 9-0, and a little more than a month later sat at an unprecedented 35-5 after 40 games. In October, they boat-raced an overwhelmed San Diego Padres squad to roll to a four-games-to-one World Series title, the fourth in franchise history. Would the city's residents come together as they did nearly two decades earlier in a moment of solidarity and joy? This is a chapter about fans behaving badly, so no. No, they did not. The celebration following the Tigers victory in 1984 still ranks among the most unruly in sports history more than 30 years later. Fans partied around the old ballpark into the wee hours of the morning. Even in the early hours, however, it was clear that the night presented a vastly different aura than that of the joyous celebration following the 1968 title. Old footage shows local news reporters struggling to deliver their live reports as masses of drunken revelers crowded around and clamored for airtime. The lasting image of the crowning achievement of 1980s Detroit Tigers baseball remains to this day a photograph of 17-year-old Kenneth "Bubba" Helms. In the wildest of wild moments, an intrepid photographer immortalized young Helms raising a World Series pennant in front of an overturned police car engulfed in flames. The celebration claimed one life and led to several dozen arrests. Eight women were raped, and the property damage ran into the millions. A beautiful moment for Tigers fans transformed into an ugly moment for humanity.

"People try to explain it in a lot of different ways," Silverman said, as he did his part to explain why fans in Detroit tore their city apart in 1984. "In Detroit, a lot of it was linked back to the timing of the game, the length of time between championships, and the mix of fans who were there after the game. The other things to consider are how the police prepare for and handle fans; there's a balance between being too lenient and overly confrontational that [if out of balance] can also incite violence in cities. In the case of Detroit in 1984, there might have been a case of over-response by the police, which inflamed the situation."

After the terrorist attacks on the World Trade Center and the Pentagon in 2001, an advertising campaign rolled out to serve as a deterrent. The campaign featured the tagline, "If you see something, say something," and advertising creative blanketed the New York City subway system. During that time, I recalled a shift in out-of-home advertising – in subway cars, on roadside billboards and draped across skyscrapers in midtown Manhattan. The shift went from an image of a single bag left on an empty subway car to a quilt of close-up images of people's eyes staring out from the advertisements. You don't need a visual of a mysterious bag to know to what the message referred. "If you see something, say something." More apt, perhaps: "We're watching you." This recalibration proved purposeful and effective. Similar campaigns run on a much smaller scale when the requisite call-to-action involves honor system payments. Whatever the scenario, direction to pay in this method often comes with an image of a person or, again, a pair of eyes, staring forward with a suspicious glare that says, "Do the right thing." Even at my office, the kitchen sink is guarded by a picture of a pair of eyes to make sure employees wash their dirty dishes. The reason for this is simple: behavior improves when people believe someone, somewhere, is watching. Putting this concept into the context of a post-game celebration, a noticeable police presence during these moments can have a similar effect on crowds. Proximity and perhaps a few well-timed, purposeful glances at the rowdiest among the hordes of revelers might keep these moments from spiraling into all-out riot mode. However, as Silverman explained, this too is a balancing act. Too loosely organized and unnoticeable and the attending police force proves incapable of keeping the action at bay. Too much police presence, coupled with a few over-anxious crowd control officers dense to the difference between joyous celebration and opportunistic rebellion, can prove equally futile at preventing disorderly conduct. In fact, the police are at times responsible for *starting* the mayhem if proven too jittery among a throng of partiers. As Silverman put it, "You don't want riot police shooting tear gas into crowds when people are just celebrating after games."

Another element at play when fans overdo it in the wake of a championship is a lack of awareness of the potential for negative outcomes to occur amid too much celebration. People react differently to stimulus and sometimes, the output devolves into something sinister that's far more damaging than a regrettable hangover. In this way, Detroit and its professional baseball franchise did itself a disservice with its lack of anticipation that a city marred by riots in the past might revert to old habits if given the opportunity.

"In other cities that I've lived in where there have been championships followed by vandalism and property damage and fights, the franchises and police departments in the city have had PR campaigns to tell people to celebrate responsibly," Silverman said, referring to a sense of awareness in cities that those with a history of rioting might riot again. "There hadn't been anything happening in Detroit of that nature for years and that might have had people with their guard down and not prepared for it. The awareness that it could happen might reduce the chances that it happens – the consciousness that things could get out of hand can get people to curb their behavior a little bit."

When sports fans resort to vandalism and violence amid the post-championship glow, they do so in contradiction with what brings us together in harmonious sameness when we walk into a stadium. For three hours, the powerful force of fandom overshadows any differences that might otherwise polarize a pair of strangers sitting side-by-side for an evening. The great unifier, the flames of group love stoked by our favorite sports franchises, keep us happily shielded from whatever haunts us in the outside world. When the final act is over, and our team reigns supreme, we're shot like a cannonball back into real life. Our differences, ambiguous and immaterial just moments before, reveal themselves again and the rest of our persona bubbles to the surface for better or worse. As Silverman mentioned, postgame riots occur due to a complex stew of circumstances. When the game ends, the goodwill and positivity also ends. Perhaps fueled by an excess of alcohol continuing deep into the witching hours, differences lead to tension. Frustrations from everyday life that people had checked at the door now return and spill over into the streets, leaving the host city susceptible to all kinds of brutality.

"In the early '90s when the Chicago Bulls won World Championships, there were a few different times where there was rioting, looting, and vandalism that happened after those championships," Silverman said. "It happened in L.A. with the Los Angeles Kings hockey championship in 2012 … It happens in a lot of cities – it's not something unique to Detroit. You might link the over-celebration to other frustrations in the cities. Maybe a slow economy or uneven investment that's taking place in communities so while people are both happy and celebrating, there are opportunities available to do vandalism. It just depends on the particular situation with each game and the type of celebration that happens."

13
THE COSTUMING CRAZE

I had settled into my seat just beyond the Oakland Athletics dugout when I heard it for the first time. At first, it emerged as a faint noise, nearly indistinguishable from the many familiar sounds of a live ballgame. Then, it began emanating from every direction at once. I took a sip from a cold adult beverage, leaned back to watch a few players fall into their pre-game routine of running drills and stretches and then there it was again, twang-twang-twang. A quick peek over my shoulder proved inconclusive as families filed down to their seats and vendors hawked their wares – *CHURROS! Get 'yer CHURROS here!* Then suddenly, *TWANG-TWANG!* The sound crept closer, little by little. Finally I could hear a raspy voice bouncing off the rows of empty seats surrounding me. These empty seats are typical at this hour, as I do and always will enjoy spending a little extra time in the stadium before the first pitch and before the masses roll in to fill the section. My focus on the pregame warm-ups was interrupted by a definitive and repetitive mantra droning into the evening air, "We're number one! We're number one!" In an instant, there he was: Banjo Man.

The first thing I noticed was the beard. The mostly gray beard – which I now know he had long before I enjoyed my first visit to the Coliseum – was both impressive and unkempt. This man stood before me like a modern day

Santa Claus yelling out, "We're number one! We're number one!" even as he settled in the row of seats just behind me. He looked tired, but he also looked content as he sang along with the humming strings. Some find this pre-game performance and daily ritual pleasing – on that day, with his eyes closed and a smile sweeping across his face, a song resonating from his lips, Banjo Man was most pleased of all. Clutching his banjo, he completed his super-fan look with a green and gold cape, Athletics T-shirt, khaki pants and, gracing a salt-and-pepper mane to match his glorious beard, a delightful little propeller hat. A few quick strums of his banjo, indecipherable lyrics, and another reminder of our position (number one, if you had forgotten) and then he was off. Banjo Man flew back up the stairs toward the concourse, cape flapping in the breeze. He roamed slowly through the concourse, strumming and posing for pictures with fans as they entered for a night of baseball. He might have whispered, "Go A's" as they turned to leave. Or he might have just kept strumming and shuffling on his way.

The man who plays Banjo Man, Stacy Samuels, is a man of mystery. Before his daily stadium march, Samuels had been a successful executive (his propeller hat business, Interstellar Propellers, has sold more than 1.5 million hats at last count). Now in his mid-60s, Samuels has become a fixture at A's home games and even a few 49ers football games. A rousing chorus of, "Banjo Man!" follows him wherever he goes in and around the ballpark. His act elicits an equal mix of smiles from supporters and skepticism from those who refuse to believe the shtick is real. The vitriol is most potent from those fans that have had the misfortune of seeing this typically green-and-gold clad musician in the sea of orange and black at San Francisco Giants games. Oakland fans don't often forgive transgressions like this, but as for me, I try to forgive and forget.

163

In any case, wherever he may roam, Banjo Man looks the part of baseball's quirky super-fan tradition. Of course, he is not alone with his over-the-top act, one that comes complete with props and musical accompaniment. Stick with an Athletics game long enough and you'll begin to hear the rhythmic thumping emanating from a collective of talented drummers seated in the bleachers, spanning from left field all the way to right. You might even see a handful of costumed drummers – including a man dressed from head to toe in green spandex – circling the stadium in an effort to stir up some cheers for the hometown ball club. I'm a simple man, and I'm much more comfortable kicking back with a little sustenance in a section within range of home plate. I'll support my team with a hat and shirt – occasionally a jersey. That's the far reach of my apparel collection, as I have yet to entertain such bold clothing considerations as strapping on a cape or squeezing myself into some other loud expression of my fandom. But they're out there – boy, are they out there. And not just in Oakland either, though we do aim for a unique level of weirdness out here on the West Coast. These costumed noisemakers can be found at every stadium in every city and across every sport and, by virtue of their larger-than-life personas, they are not too hard to find. But are they simply attention-starved amateur entertainers or are they diehard fans, as much as anyone else, finding creative ways to root on their favorite teams? What compels fans to bring props to the game? Have these fans been part of baseball all along or did they spring out of a particular era? All due respect to Banjo Man and his ilk, but do some of these costumed fans perhaps have a few screws loose? These questions roll through my mind whenever the Athletics' resident propeller-head pops into my section or whenever I hear those drums pounding away beyond the outfield wall. Don't get me wrong – I love every bit of it because, through my own 30-year history with baseball, the ballpark character seemed to be an ever-present reality. But I'm peeling back the layers of the onion here and feeling my way along the path toward what makes fans tick. Surely if that's the goal, then it's necessary to understand the history that led to the arrival of this motley crew of misfits that march to a different tune.

These questions led me to John Thorn, who has held the distinction of Official Baseball Historian for Major League Baseball since the 2011 season. My hope when we first met was that Thorn, a studious observer and archivist of the game of baseball, could unearth for me a piece of lore I had been struggling to track down. Maybe he had allowed his gaze to stray from the field of play and its outcomes just enough to catch a glimpse of the characters roaming the crowd. And in these diversions, perhaps a few stories about the creation and evolution of diehard fandom over the years would come tumbling into view. I came to Thorn a desperate and puzzled man. I was on the hunt for the origin story of these quirky ballpark characters and perspective on what might inspire fans to wear – quite literally – their fandom on their sleeve. As it turns out, Thorn had found the fan experience to be just as captivating as I had. Only, Thorn left little doubt about his feelings toward the weird and wacky clown division of our diehard fraternity. The caped crusaders of our sporting cathedrals don't carry much credence for baseball's foremost expert.

"These [costume-clad fans] are all certifiable. No particular respect should be accorded the super-fan. The super-fan is not super in anything except losing," Thorn said. Well then. At this moment of our conversation, I feel compelled to reassure Thorn that I counted myself among the scorecard-wielding super-fans and not the costumed crazies in order to prevent the discussion from going in a horribly hostile direction. You and me, John – we're in this together! "Baseball, football and basketball to a lesser extent – hockey hardly at all – have encouraged stockbrokers and lawyers to act like Mardi Gras revelers. For three hours they get a pass. They can get themselves good and roaring drunk and behave in a way that they could not anywhere but the arena," Thorn said.

Experience informs his point of view. For much of his life, he has studied the ever-changing game of baseball. The one constant from era to era remains the oddballs that come out of the woodwork to inflict on everyone else their desire to be seen and heard. "They're exhibitionists," he continued. "They're not permitted to be exhibitionists in the real world for fear of arrest."

No, John Thorn is not a fan of the demonstrative variety of super-fans. He is not a fan of them at today's ballgames and he would not have been a fan of them during early 20th century ballgames either. He has researched them, however – begrudgingly or otherwise – and traces their origin back to a group of rowdy rabble-rousers in the 1890s. The Royal Rooters, as they were called, scored their own special seating section at the home games of the Boston Braves National League club. From this perch, they would shower the team with support and make life generally unpleasant for all within earshot. When the team left town for road trips, the Rooters would follow. It all came apart, however, over a dispute regarding their seating arrangement. This disagreement led to the entire outfit transferring their loyalty (the first known bandwagon fans?) to the new American League club – known then and now as the Boston Red Sox – in 1901. Now, the real fun had begun. The unit banged drums, blew whistles, played horns and just generally had a jolly good time rooting on professional ball's newcomers. "They were famous, exhibitionistic fans who became celebrated for annoying all of those around them," Thorn said.

Tripp Whitbeck, a 33-year-old Washington Nationals diehard and costume aficionado, might take issue with Thorn's assessment. After all, the man widely hailed by fans and ballpark staff alike as the Mayor of NatsTown is nothing if not a loyal fan of the red, white, and blue. That is, the Nationals, though I imagine it might apply to his feelings about America too. The Mayor of NatsTown, however, has a shtick. He wears red wigs and white gloves. He wears Uncle Sam hats and red sequined jackets. Yes, he has a trademark "act." Funny enough, he studied law and had been a real estate development attorney before pursuing a new career in sales. Perhaps there is something to Thorn's "Mardi Gras revelers" description of stockbrokers and lawyers after all.

"There's this thing I started doing the last couple of years that I call the Tripp Homerun Trot where every time a Nats player hits a homerun, as politely as I can I ask the people to my left to get up so I can run by them. And [then] I run down the front aisle along the field and high-five fans and run all the way back," he proudly explained. He then shared how his stroll along the outer edges of the field started without the team having even hit a homerun. Rather, what would become a telegraphed move for years to come began as an honest to goodness, wholly natural and unscripted outburst of pure joy expressed by this cos-tumed-clad bandit sitting by himself in section 135. "We were down by about nine runs at one point and by God when we hit a double to take the lead and we went up 10-9, I was so excited and no one was there that I just got up and ran, and then the people that were there hanging out gave me high-fives as I went by. Then the next day we hit a big home run and I said, 'Screw it, I'll just run again.' That was probably the most joyful moment I've ever had."

Whitbeck serves as an interesting case study for anyone trying to understand what motivates diehard fans and, furthermore, what drives fans to dress like every game is Halloween. Intelligent, articulate, and charismatic, Whitbeck bucks conventional thinking that ballpark characters are nothing more than attention-starved lunatics outside of their ballpark routine. He is smart, likeable, and he loves his team. Tripp's journey to becoming a ballpark character started in New York City where he had initially been a lifelong fan of the New York Mets. Switching allegiances within the same division, the NL East, might be considered taboo by most unofficial rules of fandom. In Whitbeck's case, once he started taking in games at Nationals Park – at first, to see the visiting Mets – his rooting interest slowly switched dugouts. He became more and more familiar with the home team and identified with its players, the fan experience, and his new second home. His passion for Nationals baseball flourished during the dreadful pre-Harper / pre-Strasburg era that saw the team selecting first or near the top in the annual amateur draft several years in a row. Such a distinction serves as a consolation prize for being perennial bottom-dwellers. Even while bearing witness to back-to-back 100-loss seasons in the early days of his Nationals fandom, Whitbeck was hooked. As is customary among fans, he cites those years of bad baseball and poor attendance as almost a badge of honor. "I was literally the only fan in my section," he recalls proudly of his early years at Nationals Park. "Maybe 100 rows and I was the only person there, but I was still having a good time." During this time, and due to his fervor for the Nationals in spite of mounting losses and amid a sea of empty seats, a stadium vendor came up with the distinction that continues to follow Whitbeck to this day.

"The vendors gave me the nickname, 'The Mayor of NatsTown.' It was like, 'Hey man, you're the only person in this section. You're like the mayor here.' And then the next day they'd say, 'Hey mayor.' And then the next day, 'Hey mayor – it's the Mayor of NatsTown, everyone!' It happened organically and ever since then I've had such a good time that that's where the loyalty grew out of. It wasn't necessarily something that was born into me, although spirit was something that was born into me. I've always been a team spirit kind of guy."

That's putting it mildly. As a high school student, Whitbeck supported the varsity football team on Friday nights by painting his body red even as the team fell short more often than not. At Amherst College, the color scheme changed to purple, but the action was the same. Before long, he was parading around as the school mascot – not unlike his current role as the spiritual leader and unofficial mascot for the Nationals. For Whitbeck, the transformation from a casual fan to all-in ballpark character started simply enough in the third row of section 135 at Nationals Park. First, he purchased an innocuous Nationals hat to help blend in with the rest of the fan community. Then shortly afterward, he bought his first Nationals jersey. And then one day, he got a crazy idea.

"When I bought a red and white wig, people responded really well to it. They wanted to take pictures and they would give me a high-five and say, 'Hey man, that looks great.' We had a losing team on the field so it was kind of nifty to have someone who cared," he said of his first foray into unconventional costuming. "One of the beauties of the Internet is that you can get a lot of cheap crap from China. Everything I have is about three dollars. And then it just metastasized into buying more and more fun silly stuff and then as I became well known and as the team started playing better, I just decided to up my game a little bit and researched a little bit online what it would take to get a sequined suit made. Who doesn't, right?

"I found a purveyor in Thailand who, if you sent your measurements to her and told her what color you wanted, would send it in a banged up DHL box. It just kind of happens, it wasn't really a conscious choice. I tend to be one of those people who when I do something I do it very, very all the way."

There are exhibitionistic fans and there are real, loyal diehards, according to Thorn. As I spoke with Whitbeck, it became apparent to me that sometimes, we wear both hats – literally. While Thorn and I ping-ponged from one example of the former to the other, I was convinced he had never met a fan quite like the Mayor of NatsTown. This made me wonder about the type of fan he did hold in high regard. And then he told me a story about a woman who attended every Red Sox home game through the 1930s and 1940s. "She was acknowledged by Ted Williams on a daily basis at home. She was a super fan. You can be a super fan in terms of your devotion, you don't have to be an exhibitionist."

As we continued our discussion, this idea of loyalty bubbled to the forefront. In Thorn's eyes, fans he deemed worthy of respect were those that displayed their fandom through quiet dedication and reverence for the performing athletes. This behavior is in stark contrast to those who fancy themselves the loudest guy in the bar or the most obnoxious person in the grandstands. I suppose that isn't surprising, considering Thorn has dedicated a lifetime to the game of baseball and has strengthened his bonds through a studious pursuit of knowledge about our national pastime. Thorn, born in a displaced persons camp in the American sector of occupied Germany, credits baseball with encouraging his adjustment to the American way of life after crossing the sea at the tender age of two. As a German-speaking child, he discovered early that a nickel for a pack of baseball cards made for a worthwhile investment. For a small price, he learned that he could accelerate his adoption of the English language and acceptance into the broader community of sports-minded, card-crazy youth. Blessed with an uncanny memory, young John Thorn wowed the neighborhood kids in those days with his ability to recite statistics and factoids popular with the early Topps trading card packs. At the age of five, an unbreakable bond between a self-proclaimed "fat little German kid" and baseball was born. He would grow to spend the formative years of his life as a Brooklyn Dodgers fan and continue to stick with his childhood fascination for another decade. He did so even after they famously left New York for the sunny skies of Southern California. However, it wouldn't be too long before a shiny new local team would capture his attention and begin to cultivate a fresh relationship that would sustain through present day. Thorn can recall the precise moment during a 1965 ballgame when his allegiance shifted from Dodgers blue to the expansion Metropolitans as he watched the Dodgers' Sandy Koufax square off against the Mets Tug McGraw. Similar to Whitbeck's transition from the Mets to the Nationals, Thorn found that he had begun to pull for the Mets by mid-game. His rooting instincts had changed in the course of one game, and as he would remind me later regarding my own bi-coastal rooting interests, "You've got to remember where your feet are." His feet were in New York and his heart now belonged to the New York Mets. For nearly a century and a half, the act of identifying with local teams, even if requiring the transition of loyalty from one team to another, has proven to be core to our DNA as sports fans and as an evolving society.

"In the 1870s and 1880s, when new towns were springing up, one of the ways to identify your town as being on the map was forming a ball club and playing against other clubs for honor. If you really wanted to win, you might pay a little extra to bring a ringer into town and change his name," Thorn said. "Winning became important and then the question is, what is it about winning that felt so good? Now we get to the core of fandom: vicarious success, life lived through another. You live and you die with the fortunes of others and in the end, they don't matter. For the weak-minded, it becomes all-important. Your team cannot lose – it must not lose. But of course, baseball is a great teacher of life. In baseball as it is in life, it's more about losing than it is about winning."

I began to understand as our conversation evolved the depth of Thorn's connection to baseball. If I love baseball, and I do, I was speaking to a man whose fandom was rooted in something even more meaningful than my run-of-the-mill diehard origin story. Thorn does not just enjoy baseball. He is grateful for baseball. He has remained loyal to baseball because baseball is loyal to him. "The idea that I was going to attach myself to baseball or that baseball was going to attach itself to me seemed a constant in my life," he said. "And baseball has been a constant in my life from the time I was three to my days of being a grandfather.

"If there is a greater super fan than I, I don't know who that person would be. I have my favorite team, but I follow all of baseball. I follow it from the 18th century to last night's ESPN highlights. All of it is a really rich and fulfilling tapestry," he explained. "I have the great privilege and honor of calling baseball my profession, as well as my hobby. I have the very odd experience of working hard at my computer for 8 to 10 hours and finally saying, 'I am exhausted from this.' And then I go downstairs and get a cold one out of the fridge and watch a ballgame. Profession and hobby are one, which makes for a constant in life."

Thorn has a beautifully poetic way with words as he describes his life's passion. He is nothing if not a storyteller, and baseball provides a rich well of content from which to draw from. But enough about that. I came to Thorn for an origin story, and by God, I was going to get my origin story. At this stage of our conversation, we have already ruled out most costumed weirdos as authentic die-hard fans. We can thank the Royal Rooters for paving the way for today's sideshow characters that grace the world's ballparks. So what about the rest of us? When did being a "fan" first become a term to describe the gaggle of observers staring at grown men playing with bats and balls?

"There are famous fans throughout history and there is the interesting derivation of the very term fan. Its origin is a bit of a mystery," Thorn said, much to my dismay. "There is the idea that it's short for fanatic, which is conceptually pleasing, but I am thinking probably incorrect. Historian Peter Morris had the interesting theory, which he backed up pretty well that it comes from the paper fans that bleacherites would use to cool themselves in the 1880s. The flapping of their tongues has been likened to the whirring of a fan and that seems to me the best possible explanation. One of the great pleasures of being a fan is to share your opinions at the ballpark with the people around you. Your opinions might not be worth very much to the player, but it could make for pleasingly contentious talk."

Talk about your all-time letdowns. On one hand, the beginnings of the sport of baseball are equally left to interpretation as questions abound among people who care to debate such a thing. Did Army General Abner Doubleday dream up what would become the sport of baseball while in Cooperstown, New York? Did Americans fashion a game of their own based loosely on the rules and action of foreign games like cricket? No one knows for sure, but even if mere creation myth, these explanations at least offer some generally pleasing payoff. The former, touting Doubleday as the creator of baseball in the now home of the Baseball Hall of Fame, serves as a sentimental favorite. The latter delivers a much more practical explanation while still providing naval-gazing Americans with the right to claim that if Americans did not develop baseball, at least they improved cricket. For fans, there is no such story. Our tongues flap like fans and so we shall be dubbed, "fans." Can it really be as straightforward as that? After sharing this likely origin of the term fan, used to describe the mouth-agape onlookers beyond the white lines of those late-nineteenth century ball fields, Thorn went on to explain that the athletes they watched, in fact, derided the ancient ancestors of present-day fans. As he told it, the waving of fans en masse, which later turned into the whirring of motorized fans, tended to offer distraction and annoyance to the uniformed men on the field. My goodness, could this get any worse? Fellow fans, we sound terrible. It started to make sense once I allowed that idea to marinate awhile – that flapping tongues equated to fans and that, in turn, related to me in the present day. After all, quite a few of my team color-clad brethren make quite a commotion as they cheer on their favorite team. And even I can count several times that I have come home at the end of an exciting ballgame having lost my voice. So be it. I can come to grips with being a tongue-flapper. That's all part of the experience.

"It's all fun to me," Whitbeck concluded when we began to discuss what kind of benefit he gets out of spending most evenings and some days sitting at the ballpark in a goofy outfit. "I anticipate, assuming I can afford it, coming out whether the team is losing 100 games or whether the team is winning 100 games. That's what I was doing back in 2009 and that's what I'm doing now. For me, it's the fun. It's the experience."

14
BASEBALL HEAVEN

St. Louis is a quiet city, a sprawl of brick buildings and little green parks nestled within the even broader sprawl of St. Louis County. The Gateway to the West, boasting one of the country's most beautiful architectural wonders in the Gateway Arch, offers little in the way of the block-to-block entertainment you might find in other major cities and even less in terms of casual interaction with other people within the arteries of its downtown community. There is a dearth of things to do here, St. Louis lifer and board member of the St. Louis Browns Historical Society Emmett McAuliffe had told me once. I would wager that, if one were so inclined, one might walk straight from the muddy banks of the Mississippi River right through the heart of the city without making contact with another living soul. I say this with confidence because that is precisely what I did one sticky summer night during a tour through Missouri's great baseball cities. Indeed, for all it might want for action in other facets of life, St. Louis is nothing if not a great baseball city.

There was a time when St. Louis sat among the nation's most important cities in terms of a bustling populace, industrial firepower, and straight up action. During this era, St. Louis also served as the key chess move during strategic planning for the Major League Baseball's American League, which was a fledgling professional baseball organization built to contend head-to-head with the still young National League. At the turn of the 20th century, American League founder Ban Johnson began to cobble his league together by transforming a Milwaukee-based team from the Western League into the St. Louis Browns. This would be the first in a series of strategic decisions made to ensure the composition of a new league had a stronghold in all of the nation's most important cities. The Orioles moved to New York to become the fabled Yankees. Funny enough, the Browns would relocate to Baltimore 50 years later to create the Orioles all over again and to this day, the Orioles hardly acknowledge their Midwestern roots. The Athletics emerged as perennial contenders in North Philadelphia. In Boston, Red Sox Nation would begin their rise to icon status as the Boston Americans. Johnson continued to fill in the gaps here and there, but these were the key moves. Four teams in America's four most impressive cities. The crown jewel of the "Show Me" state, St. Louis, launched into a new century with enough momentum to support two professional baseball teams. Of course St. Louis needed two pro ball clubs – how could it not?

Unfortunately, not all superpowers stand the test of time and St. Louis' status, along with its population, suffered one gut punch after another as the years rolled along. Following World War II, the city endured a long, slow decline similarly damaging to what its Rust Belt brethren felt during that same period, and watched its population slip away since its peak somewhere north of 850,000 in the 1950s. Today, slightly more than 300,000 people call the city home – not enough to crack the nation's top 50 cities, and a long fall from the days when St. Louis served as a vital cog of America's growth as a nation.

To put the city's precipitous population dip into context, the 2010 U.S. Census counted a massive migration of nearly 30,000 residents out of St. Louis across the previous 10-year period – an eight percent slip. Local politicians and city leaders point to myriad reasons for the decline. I find it hard to believe that a single, isolated cause accounts for a dip so significant. Rather, some combination of factors has led some 500,000 people to make their way somewhere else – anywhere else. Some point to a slow-to-recover local economy while others speculate about the impact of a broad desire among residents to move closer to jobs outside of the city. Then sadly, questions began to emerge about "white flight." The broader county of St. Louis, while losing 10 percent of its white population, increased its black population by 21 percent. More telling, in my esti-mation, is the disappearance of more than 22,000 young people under the age of 17 during those 10 years – repre-senting more than 75 percent of the mass exodus. On the surface, this serves as a damning indictment of the city's school system. In some ways, however, we have stepped back in time: the streets of St. Louis, while contemporized for the modern world, boast a populace tally closer to post-Civil War times than mid-20th century boom times.

Amid this startling decline, however, remained the beating heart at the city's core that for more than a century pumped life and energy into an otherwise sleepy town. St. Louis, once a dynamic, two-team city and now host city to the Cardinals exclusively, is Baseball Heaven.

When Jim Edmonds, a centerfielder who made a name for himself with the Cardinals in the early 2000s, joined the team at the turn of the 21st century, slugger Mark McGwire greeted his new teammate with a phone call and a cry of, "Welcome to Baseball Heaven!" It's dif-ferent here, McGwire assured his new teammate. On that spring day, he was not the first to make that association. For years, fans and players alike have proudly proclaimed this modest city with a waning population and deafeningly quiet neighborhoods the center of the baseball universe. So we must ask the question: is it?

"St. Louis fans are some of the most passionate baseball fans I've seen in all of the sport. I've been to several games in St. Louis, but there was one particular experience that really brought it home for me," said Bob Kendrick, President of the Negro Leagues Baseball Museum, an absolute gem in Kansas City, located some 250 miles west. "The late, great Buck O'Neil and I were going down to St. Louis for an event with the Cardinals and we were there on a Thursday get-away day Businessman's Special where they were playing the Cincinnati Reds. At that time, Ken Griffey was still on the team, but the Reds were not really a good team and yet 35,000 people were at the ballpark that day. For a Businessman's Special on get-away day that cemented in my mind what a great baseball town this is."

The Miami Marlins, discussed in an earlier chapter, dream about one day enjoying the ticket office success of the St. Louis Cardinals. In 1997, the Cardinals lost 89 games while drawing 2.6 million fans through its turnstiles. Two years later, they finished 21.5 games out of first place and still drew 3.2 million. The team has not drawn less than 2 million fans in a season not impacted by labor disputes since 1980. To be clear, the Cardinals have typically produced winning ball clubs, but unlike many other cities, winning is not the only recipe for box office success. Of course, it would be wildly superficial to crown Cardinals fans as the best fans in baseball simply because they show up. The Los Angeles Dodgers typically outdraw the Cardinals, but more people would be inclined to identify Dodgers fans as late to arrive and early to leave than they would label them the game's best support system for our million-dollar heroes on the playing field (you can make a strong argument that Dodgers fans get a bad rap). Showing up is not enough – there must be something else brewing in St. Louis besides beer for the masses and easily impressed fans. McAuliffe, a man dedicated to preserving his city's legacy as a two-team town and a veritable encyclopedia of local knowledge, does, in fact, attribute some of the city's baseball tradition to those golden suds.

"St. Louis was a Catholic and High Lutheran town and Chris Vonderahe [owner of the St. Louis Brown Stockings, which eventually became the Cardinals] was the first tavern owner to own a team," he explained. "The American Association that Chris Vonderahe's team dwelled in was sometimes ridiculed as the beer and whiskey league. They also played on Sunday, so you had this divide very early on between Puritan America and non-Puritan America as represented by the ones that drank beer and the ones that didn't. Then you've got St. Louis: a little more rough and tumble, a few more cowboy Western types, but a huge amount of German Lutherans, and French and Irish Catholics that what they wanted to do on Sunday was drink a beer and watch a game. They were allowed to do that here and I think somehow that got built into our core in a way that it didn't get built into other cities' cores."

I thought spending time elbow to elbow with the Cardinals faithful – those beer-swilling Catholics and Lutherans that McAuliffe had described – during a hot summer evening in July might reveal the magic of what makes this place so special in the eyes of so many. As much as I enjoyed the games played within the confines of Busch Stadium, and as pleasant as it might have been to talk baseball with my red-clad neighbors, the game experience did not lead me closer to answers for what makes St. Louis unique. The teams entertained, the home crowd cheered and then we all relocated for post-game entertainment to the new Ballpark Village, installed before the 2014 season as a loud, excessive party spot just outside the stadium gates.

Rather, to understand St. Louis as a baseball town, I had to wait until the crowds cleared. I had to wait until the stadium lights dimmed and the streets of St. Louis transformed back into the barren wasteland of lifelessness that I had experienced earlier in my trip. Along those desolate streets, what the city left me with as I made my way around the exterior of the ballpark in near darkness were a handful of life-sized statues speckled along the walk around the stadium grounds. They served as miniature reminders that this once-great city still held a richness of character and cultural relevance that commanded respect. Lou Brock. Ozzie Smith. Bob Gibson. Cool Papa Bell. History, but a different kind of history. Baseball history in St. Louis weaves together with our own history as an imperfect, yet continually improving, society.

"It speaks to the baseball lore that has been a part of that city for quite some time," Kendrick said in reference to the unique cultural awareness alive at the center of the city's fan community, which now focuses wholly on the Cardinals. "Fans in St. Louis have seen great baseball for a long time, both black and white. During that era of segregation, you had the Negro Leagues operating in St. Louis, and it goes back to 1920 in an organized capacity with the old St. Louis Giants who eventually became the St. Louis Stars. That helped shape the overall baseball experience in St. Louis."

If you are a St. Louis baseball fan – not specifically the Cardinals, but rather, of baseball in its entirety as it has played out within city limits through the years – there exists an honest appreciation for the athletes that have come before even with the focus on the present-day action. You can feel it in the air when you enter Busch Stadium, but you can also literally stumble into it as you head home after a game. Fans share pride in the fact that this city, in contrast with newer baseball towns like Denver or Seattle, has experienced baseball both as entertainment and also as an active driver for addressing broader cultural issues. Even St. Louis' least successful franchise, the since-departed Browns that McAuliffe honors so dearly, played a role in integrating baseball's premier league while building a strong baseball culture long before the likes of Ozzie Smith and Albert Pujols came and went.

"Even though the St. Louis Browns weren't a very good baseball team, they certainly play a pivotal role in that whole integration process with guys like Willard Brown and Hank Thompson helping to integrate the Browns and it certainly was a part of the baseball experience in St. Louis," Kendrick explained. "While the Cardinals were a little bit slow in bringing black players, man, when they did they brought some good ones."

We reminisced awhile about the old-timers that helped shape the game during the past half-century or more. Kendrick has the enviable task of marrying his personal love of America's national pastime with his professional interest of keeping the stories of the talented black ballplayers from segregated America alive for future generations to enjoy. This struck me as an extraordinarily pleasant approach to making your way through life. As a child growing up in rural Crawfordville, Georgia, Kendrick latched onto baseball at the tender age of five by teaching himself to read the box scores that ran in local papers. Crawfordville lacked the human capital necessary to field a formal hardball league, so Kendrick and his peers had to improvise. Armed with bats fashioned from tree branches and rubber balls not quite like the perfectly crafted pearly white rawhide and laced red twine of the real thing, the kids of Crawfordville would grab whatever neighborhood kids were around and hit the sandlot like their heroes. As is customary in these scenarios, Kendrick would wrap his hands around the knotty makeshift bat, close his eyes and emulate the batting style of his homerun hitting heroes. For Kendrick, it would always be the man destined to become Major League Baseball's all-time homerun champion in the mid-1970s: Hammerin' Hank Aaron. "Even today, for me, no one will ever be better than the great Henry Aaron. It goes all the way back to my childhood as a baseball fan and I honestly had no idea that I would ever make my living in baseball."

It is fortuitous that he did ultimately dedicate his professional life to furthering baseball history, since it led him to an unforgettable encounter with his childhood hero. "I got the assignment of touring Hank Aaron through the Negro Leagues Museum," he said, and I could sense the excitement in his voice as he retold a story he must have shared a thousand times. "I was reduced to that 12-year-old when he broke the record and I was in my mother's house when he's circling the bases, I'm circling the bases with him. The couch was first base, the television was second base, there was another little couch on the other side of the room – that was third base – and a little recliner was home plate. Anytime I'm in his midst I'm reduced to that 12-year-old kid again. Afterwards, Hank Aaron, his wife, and I were eating barbeque ribs up in the conference room of the Gem Theater. For me, the day can't get any better than that."

As he shared the account of this private moment he had enjoyed with one of the sport's larger than life legends, I began to realize that our conversation about Baseball Heaven – that which is synonymous with the city of St. Louis – had begun to pinball between the hundreds of miles of I-70 linking St. Louis and Kansas City. We were back in the historic 18th and Vine district, walking the streets and, metaphorically speaking, stepping back in time. Passing the legendary Blue Room jazz club on the left, skipping across the street to another historic landmark, the Gem Theater, and dining on Kansas City's saucy barbeque ribs with a baseball legend. That's when I knew that while St. Louis may serve as the headquarters of Baseball Heaven, angelic sister cities exist anywhere bats are swinging – and particularly so if they've been swinging bats for generations.

"It's the myth and the lore and the legend surrounding the likes of guys like Satchel Paige, Cool Papa Bell and Josh Gibson because you only really have the great accounts of the feats that these men were able to accomplish," he said of the powerful draw he feels every time he walks through the halls of his own museum. "That adds to the mystique that surrounds the Negro Leagues, and when you couple all of that with our national pastime, you can see why people love this story. For me to have a hand in trying to ensure the long-term future of this organization, and to have worked side-by-side with the great Buck O'Neil [prior to his death, O'Neil helped to build what is now an institution for baseball fans who visit Kansas City], all of that is significant to me. It is Baseball Heaven in many senses."

Kendrick makes his living shining a light – for guests like Henry Aaron at one end of the spectrum and baseball fans like myself at the other – on the excellence exhibited by a collection of athletes that, for most of the world, would otherwise live on in anonymity. I was glad that during our discussion, Kendrick chose to call out Cool Papa Bell. Bell, celebrated for his speed and uncanny ability to track down everything hit within range (and beyond normal range) in centerfield, has long been my favorite Negro League star since I first became familiar with baseball's forgotten pros. If not for Kendrick, O'Neil and the efforts of Kansas City's little pearl of a museum, his exploits might live on as a mere footnote in baseball history and for most, a forgotten man somewhere on the long list of Negro League players that never received their shot at the Majors by the time its doors opened to black athletes. There is, however, one city that never forgets the damage Bell inflicted on the base paths (Bell is alleged to have stolen two bases on one pitch at one time or another during his heyday) and in the outfield. In St. Louis, where Bell starred for the aptly named St. Louis Stars in the 1920s and 1930s and where his statue stands today outside of the Busch Stadium gates, the man's accomplishments are legendary. This city remembers and appreciates its stars. "Lou Brock talks about Cool Papa Bell with such great reverence and how he taught him things about base stealing," Kendrick said, as he described the scene at Bell's statue dedication ceremony that brought fans from all over St. Louis to a little stretch of sidewalk in front of the Cardinals' mammoth ballpark. "He would say things like, 'Cool Papa, I never learned that,' and Cool Papa's response was, 'It ain't in the book.'"

Kendrick followed that story with another about Hall of Fame hurler Bob Gibson, who made his mark on the game by recording arguably the single greatest season in big league history for the Cardinals on their way to a 1968 World Series match-up against the Detroit Tigers. That season's performance by Gibson (and a host of breakout pitching seasons by others) in turn forced Major League Baseball to lower the pitching mound by five inches to even the playing field for hitters. That's right – so dominant was Gibson that the league changed around him. As Kendrick explained to me, "Anytime you change a sport, you a bad dude."

In St. Louis, baseball is bigger than the game. Gibson's performance on the mound came during a time of civic unrest and volatile race relations in America and as such, became a cultural touchstone for an entire generation of St. Louisans. When blended with the social issues of the time, baseball took on a different meaning and served as a uniting force when outside of the stadium, people were anything but unified. "Our country was at civil unrest and much of our country was rioting. You had the King assassination, you had Kennedy assassinated and our country was in upheaval," Kendrick said. "Baseball was that unifying presence and in St. Louis, you had all of these great black stars at that time and so baseball was certainly part of our healing effect in St. Louis."

These moments shape our perspective as fans. In St. Louis, baseball fans don't simply enjoy watching games. Fans here seem to share a genuine thankfulness for the sport's role in improving life within its city limits and encouraging people, who would otherwise remain separated, to accept one another. Of course, this is not a characteristic unique to Cardinals Country. Rather, similar feelings emanate from other baseball towns that recognize the game's role in lifting their community out of hardships – if only for three hours at a time. As noted in an earlier chapter, the team that eventually upended Gibson's Cardinals, the Detroit Tigers, often receives credit for ending the riots that plagued their city during the summer of 1968. When our societal issues can be resolved by refocusing our energy on common ground, Baseball Heaven can pop up just about anywhere. For those who travel a few hours west to Kendrick's Negro Leagues Baseball Museum, you can find it in the stories of a handful of immensely talented black ballplayers who lived at the center of America's racial divide, bravely earning a living and fighting for survival in the face of great opposition.

"Most of the people who come to the museum can relate and they can grasp the pride, the passion, the perseverance and the courage that these men illustrated in the face of adversity to play this game and to play it as well as anyone had ever played it," he said. "I tell people all the time, 'What's not to love about this sport?' Because it's America at her worst, but it's also at her triumphant best."

And what of this label, Baseball Heaven? As I mentioned earlier, attending a game at Busch Stadium on a sunny day in July is at once wholly enjoyable and entirely unremarkable. It's baseball here, as beautiful and captivating as anywhere else where it takes 27 outs to complete nine innings and the team with the most runs wins the game. Aside from the view from behind home plate, which frames the Gateway Arch perfectly, the pitch-by-pitch experience is not unlike anywhere else where they might play ball. Baseball Heaven, to me, is an outdated stadium in Oakland where I witnessed the single greatest sporting moment I had ever experienced live. When Bob Kendrick strolls proudly through the rotating exhibits on display within his tiny museum nestled in a historic jazz district only slightly larger, he is in his own alcove of Baseball Heaven. And in Detroit, that moment of Baseball Heaven may have been falling into a celebratory embrace on a cold October night in 1968 with a fan from a background you hadn't expected yourself capable of accepting. Yet here you are, beginning a lifelong friendship over this mutual interest in the Detroit Tigers. Why then do we react to baseball in this way?

"The late Buck O'Neil so beautifully explained it, 'You can have two 80-year-old men sitting on the couch watching a baseball game, and a guy drops a pop fly. The first words that come out of their mouth is, 'I could have caught that,'" Kendrick said with a belly laugh. "If LeBron James misses a dunk, everybody ain't saying I could have done that!

"And I think that's the difference – it's a game we can all play and it was and is still America's favorite pastime. Baseball is a beautiful game."

15
BETTING ON LONG ODDS

While the blathering sounds of a postgame radio host bounced out of tiny transistor speakers, I narrowed my focus on a little orb of liquid set within my level tool. *Tonight, you saw just what the Athletics need to do to bring a championship to Oakland*, the host screamed across the airwaves and into my garage. I took a step back to eyeball the wall after a jitter sent the level askew. You know how these things go: a gentle tug at one end of a yardstick the tiniest fraction of an inch toward the other end, followed by the slightest nudge back in the other direction. Just as everything began to line up perfectly, on cue, my hand slipped and the process began anew. *The A's still have questions at second base – that's an obvious position of need*, the voice continued as I worked deep into the night with meticulous care. Night after night, this ritual continued while my wife shook her head in amazement and my neighbors probably wondered what the heck was going on beyond our shared patio wall. I do not claim to hold much artistic talent, but I felt like a modern day Picasso while toiling away deep into the night. My vision – my stroke of genius – revealed itself with the first brush stroke and continues its evolution to this day. The garage, a shelter for cars, would become my shrine to the game of baseball.

Excitement grew as I stenciled in the distance markers native to the O.Co Coliseum. Taking special care to space out the proper digits – 330, 367, 362, 388, and 400, respectively – along one wall and then counting back down to 330 along the next. Several layers of golden yellow atop a rich canvas of forest green. What I hoped would house my own personal celebration of our national pastime would be surrounded from end to end by the Oakland Athletics' outfield wall, accurate down to the numbering. What better way to honor the site of my greatest personal experiences with the game I loved so much? In the film "Field of Dreams," the iconic refrain of, "If you build it, they will come" echoed from the cornfields of Iowa. I was building it a few clicks west in Alameda, California. I wasn't sure if anyone would come, but I did have high hopes that the space might have new life as a home base for myself and fellow diehards. At the very least, I wanted to do right by the relics I had collected through the years. Each would have their proper place within my museum of knick-knacks and keepsakes.

If we're being honest with each other, then it is probably worth noting that my nighttime ritual of transforming the cobweb-laden dust factory that is the garage into a pristine temple of baseball goodness was my wife's idea. Or rather, it spawned from her suggestion that I put my toys in the garage. I would imagine that the deep greens stretching across two walls, along with the batting cage grass and furniture – two authentic risers from the old Veterans Stadium in Philadelphia – were not quite what she had in mind. That's superfluous now. I have my baseball-themed cave, an homage to my love of the Oakland Athletics and Philadelphia Phillies. She has a house free of bobbles. It's a win-win for everybody.

I share this story for the simple reason that, on the surface, it makes no sense. Why would I, a grown man whose time is stretched razor thin thanks to a demanding job and a growing family, sacrifice valuable sleep and

hours of my time to honor a game I will never play profes-
sionally and athletes I'll never meet? What benefit do I get
from lining up a dozen bobbleheads *just so* along a shelf
measured out with painstaking precision? I don't know if
it can be explained simply, but I do know that when I feel
the blades of grass – artificial batting cage grass, but the
fantasy is real – between my toes, I'm transported. When I
drop down into one of those bright blue plastic seats from
The Vet just as I used to do as a child, or when I switch on
the radio to catch a few innings of that evening's Athletics
game bleeding through the speakers into the night air,
the memories come flooding back. Both good and bad,
the times I have shared with the game of baseball – and
more often than not, alongside friends who feel the same
way – weave together to create a unique diehard DNA, at
once my own and shared in every way imaginable. When
I'm in this place, I flash back to the halls of Dutch Neck
Elementary School, where I had traded away most of the
highly coveted baseball card my friends wanted simply for
the chance to snag yet another worthless Von Hayes card
for my curious collection of Von Hayes cards. I'm brought
back to a cool October night when I cried alone in the
darkness of my father's living room as Joe Carter ended
the Phillies 1993 season with a World Series-ending home
run. And of course, as I scan the room and track the distance markers from one end to the other, I'm shot back in
time to every memorable experience I've lived within the
confines of the Athletics' O.co Coliseum. I remember the
final at-bat heroics and playoff celebrations, but of equal
importance in my evolution as a diehard fan, I also think
about the season-ending heartache and the Athletics' con-
tinual flirtation with the city of San Jose and the threat of
relocation.

My diehard experience is speckled with flashes in time
and this is where I come to relive those days all over again.

My brain still reserves a dusty corner for Phillies no-name Jon Zuber, who hit a two-run homerun in my first visit to Yankee Stadium where I sat among the famously rowdy bleacher creatures. I remember sneaking behind the ballpark after the game to watch future Yankees legends – Derek Jeter, Paul O'Neil, Tino Martinez, and many others – filing into the parking lot to a chorus of cheers after the game. That access is a simple pleasure of the House that Ruth Built that has been left out of the new stadium experience, but the memory is clear; those moments are alive and well in my mind even today. There is plenty of space too for the goats. Players like the nonchalant Travis Lee, who never quite fit in Philadelphia. The man who cost the Phillies a shot at a winning record in 2002 when they limped to the finish line at 80-81. You have to remember and appreciate how rare a winning record had been in those days for the Phillies. Had Lee exhibited any effort at all on a lazy foul ball, who knows what might have happened, but as it turned out, a sleepwalking catch without a throw provided a runner at third enough time to tag up and scamper home with the season-ending run. That kind of play won't make you a fan favorite in blue collar Philadelphia where we like our players at max effort and preferably covered in dirt. In any case, I sit back in my stadium seats and gently palm a baseball or take a couple short practice swings with a heavy wooden bat acquired during one of many ballpark road trips. As the creaky old seat settles into place and I slide a hand along the old metal arm rail, I'm visited by fleeting remembrances from my childhood of entering into the bright lights of cavernous Veterans Stadium from the concourse. The good and bad moments blend into the chronology of my memories; my sports experience equal parts sadness and pure joy, but all the while wholly satisfying and a part of who I am to the outside world.

"The one thing that I find interesting is that sports fans know going in that there's a 50-50 chance that this game is going to turn out bad. Maybe if they're a really good team, it's slightly better than 50-50, but the bottom line is that every fan knows that this game could turn out awful and that makes it an interesting voluntary pop culture activity," Dr. Wann had explained to me. This paradox of choosing an activity with such long odds of a positive outcome is one of the reasons he began researching fan behavior more than 30 years ago and why he continues to study and engage with diehard sports fans today. "There aren't many things that we do that we go in thinking, 'Oh yeah, after I consume this product I could be really sad. I could be really depressed for a week.' You don't go to a movie and think, 'There's a 30 percent chance that after watching this movie I'm going to want to jump off a bridge.' Sport is different in that way.

"How are there still sports fans? Because sports fans – as effectively as any group out there – have developed amazingly successful ways of coping."

We cope. We celebrate and we lament. We connect with one another and get in touch with ourselves. But most of all, we cope because those of us that have experienced the thrill that sports can deliver – those late game heroics and the anything-can-happen-and-it-just-did moments – know that if we endure tough times, the good times that come around for all of us eventually are well worth it. To hear Wann describe it, however, does make it seem insane. I have left games feeling sad and I have endured fitful nights of sleep thanks to the poor performance of my team, which is ironic because I'm sure the cadre of athletes that have let me down at one time or another slept like babies that same night. People are drawn into games for different reasons, but in the end, most of us want a taste of the same thing. The act of cheering (or booing) a sports team provides a safe haven for people to connect with the peaks and valleys of the emotional spectrum within a truncated time-frame, allowing for the release of significantly raw and honest sensations that we otherwise hold back in our civilized workaday lives. We want to feel. We want to be surrounded by like-minded people all excitedly singing from the same hymnal, and to float up and down cavernous corridors after the game hugging and high-fiving every stranger we didn't know we loved like brothers and sisters – even if just for one night. And we do because, hey, our hats and clothing match! The requisite suffering only makes the pleasure all the more enjoyable and I must say, the joy felt by 36,000 revelers during the Athletics' 2012 playoff run was likely multiplied because we had each become intimately familiar with alternating feelings of despair, sadness, and hopelessness along the road to euphoria when, earlier in the game, elimination seemed to be a virtual lock.

We are not yet aware of a diehard gene. No one telltale trait, as far as we know, drives fans to choose this quirky path – the path that leads to grand visions of a baseball-themed garage nirvana – and keeps others on the sidelines, scratching their heads. The way I see it, diehards fall in line for what I can only describe as our truest human experience. Will MacNeil, the creator of the Balfour Rage – a ritual that became a stadium-wide phenomenon in support of Athletics' closer Grant Balfour that involved vigorously pumping one's fists as if punching through a mosh pit at a metal concert – and a man who strives to attend more than 200 ballgames during a single summer, explained it well. Being at the ballpark to watch his Oakland A's while surrounded by his "summer family" is where he can truly be himself and let loose. He is no longer Will MacNeil, front desk attendant at an anonymous Bay Area hotel. Instead, he becomes the flag-waving, jersey-buying Right Field Will, every player's most dedicated supporter.

"Fans come in all shapes and sizes, all sorts of traits, all sorts of backgrounds, all kinds of characteristics and personality profiles and it really does pretty much cut across all different traits and demographics," Wann said. "At some point in the future maybe somebody will have done something that changes that conclusion, but when I find out that someone is a fan I'm never surprised because everyone can be a fan."

It's quite possible that the inclusive nature of sports is what fuels fandom and serves as a core element of the answer to the question about why fans care so much about games. After studying the topic for a long, long time, I'm convinced that we care because the games we love offer immeasurable opportunity to be included in something more than just a workforce or a family unit. At the ballpark, cheering for our likeable teams, rooting for athletes that occasionally acknowledge us, and interacting constantly with our fellow diehards, we gain a sense of inclusion not found in many of life's other pursuits. Being a sports fan is an inclusive experience because you don't have to study the craft or understand the technical detail to find something enjoyable about athletic competition. Inclusive too because sports offers an open invitation for all people to come on in and stay awhile – be entertained, make a few new friends and carry a couple memories away with you when the game ends. As Wann stated, all are welcome in the world of sports and current research does not show any one group being more likely than others to be seduced by its charms. That is an attractive proposition for anyone. It's pleasing, this idea that you can always turn on a game and enjoy the action just as much as the guy sitting next to you at a bar or in the stadium even if you wouldn't say a word to that same stranger if you happened to pass on the street. In that way, sports serves as a great equalizer with the power to strip away all of our preexisting hang-ups, stresses and prejudices that prevent people from making connections with one another. Funny enough, we're then filled with a whole new set of stresses and prejudices, though there's a degree of simplicity to these new thoughts filling our brain, and they're shared by thousands of others surrounding us in every direction: I feel anxiety that we might lose. I feel excitement that we might win. I feel love for my team. And I feel an aversion to this other team blocking our path to victory. We feel so much, good and bad, for the three or four hours when our minds are engaged in a game.

"I'm not going to call it addiction, but it [when positive things happen in sports] is a kind of reinforcement," said Dr. Sam Sommers, the Boston-based psychologist still hanging tight to his Yankees fandom in enemy territory. As an explanation for why we keep coming back to sports and the "50-50 chance we're going to be sad," as Wann had put it, Sommers reminded me that the motivation of die-hard fans is not unlike the tragic story of the laboratory mice psychologists have tormented for decades. In this, the experience of the extraordinarily unlucky mouse, our subject receives treats sporadically as continued incentive to execute an action that typically brings discomfort. "You push that lever so many times and something good comes out of it, you're going to keep pushing it."

So here we are again, back within the cement and steel of the Coliseum. The calendar reminds us that it is late September. Fervent rooters tuck in beneath the hateful tarps that dress the third deck of the stadium and surround the green and gold fans like a wreath. Postseason races are in full flight, but here in Oakland, a city that played host to some of the best baseball in the world during the previous two seasons and into July of the current year, 2014, something is different. The sea of humanity, still lively with every pitch, no longer roars with the same vigor I had grown accustomed to in these late days of the baseball season. My 3-year-old daughter, draped across my lap, sleeps peacefully as gentle applause and an occasional outburst in the stands dissipates before waking her. The excitement and enthusiasm for Oakland baseball that had become a source of pride for the region now felt deflated like a punctured balloon – slowly, yet inevitably, losing all of its air. You see, after two and a half magical years of extraordinary baseball, the Oakland Athletics will not host a playoff game and are once again playing forgettable baseball.

Let me be clear: on this day, a Sunday interleague game against the Philadelphia Phillies that closed out the final weekend series of season, the Athletics are still very much in the race. In fact, by the end of the season, the team would win *just* enough to clinch a playoff berth for the third straight season – albeit for the right to play a single game on the road in Kansas City for the newfangled all or nothing one-game Wild Card game. This race is different though, as the team limped into the postseason on a slide that saw them fall completely out of contention for the division title and left them gasping for air at the bottom of the Wild Card ranks. Indeed, a trip to the postseason required a win in the season's final game. For an emotional and dedicated fan base, closing out a season 16-31 after holding the league's best record for much of the season is a tough pill to swallow. Sadly, this is just the beginning of the turmoil that would continue to haunt every diehard Athletics fan in the long winter that followed.

As is customary, Major League Baseball releases playoff tickets for sale well before the players secure the requisite guarantee of postseason baseball. Typically, I align myself with the superstitious lot: those among us that refuse to even consider purchasing jinx-worthy postseason tickets until my team has punched their own ticket to the dance. In 2014, I broke from tradition and snapped up both the one-game Wild Card bout along with the first home game to the American League Division Series. In the event the team managed to beat the Royals, I did not intend to take my chances with the secondary market to purchase what would have been game three of a series against the rival Los Angeles Angels of Anaheim. All of this is moot, of course, since both tickets were invalid on the first day of the postseason. The A's paid a visit to Kansas City and then they went home. They quietly retreated to their own homes for months of what-ifs and what-might-have-beens. The season, once filled with so much promise and excitement, ended on a screaming liner by Salvador Perez just out of the reach of third baseman Josh Donaldson. For Athletics fans, however, it wasn't enough for the season to simply end on an extra-inning walk-off hit in a game that shouldn't have been played on the road in the first place. No, life had been much too good for Athletics fans the past few years and it was now time for the Baseball Gods to collect. The extra-inning winner only came after the A's mounted a 7-3 lead with one out in the eighth inning; after the team led 7-6 with two outs in the ninth; and after the team retook a lead it had relinquished and led 8-7 with one out in the 12th. A painful and perplexing failure to lock in a victory that the Royals appeared hell bent on giving away sent Athletics fans home from various viewing parties across the Bay Area in a state of confusion, frustration, and bemusement. Immediately following this devastating playoff exit, many people began referring to September 30 as the perfect microcosm of the 2014 season. This seems appropriate enough, but as I replayed that game in my head endlessly in the weeks that followed, I began to see that game not as a snapshot of 2014, but rather, a perfect reflection of the life of the diehard fan. In the event the Athletics managed to stave off elimination, as they had on that crisp October night in 2012 you read about in this book's first chapter, I might remember this game among the all-timers. And for Royals fans, it was indeed a night to remember forever. It was a night that captured all the emotions connected to sports fandom within a single five-hour event. Starting with an early deficit (reflection on a magical season), and then watching your team come back to take the lead (renewed hope and excitement). No, that's not enough. You need to see your team go down big late in the game (hopelessness and dread; realization that a wild ride would soon end) and then watch as your team mounts an improbable, game-tying about-face (pure joy) … before falling behind again (disgust). Royals fans know that this story has a happy ending, of course, so the most memorable moment plucked from a stew of memorable moments came at the very end: a walk-off winner to send the team to the next round (all-consuming euphoria).

As Wann explained, fans need to come to grips with the fact that their beloved sports teams fail half the time. We have a 50 percent chance of wanting to jump off a bridge after watching a ballgame. So why do we deal with the emotional toll? From where I sit – or rather, from where I stood on September 30, watching from The Englander Pub in an Oakland neighborhood while the Athletics jerked its fans around like a yo-yo – it's because even in the cruelest of defeats, the game brings people together and we get moments of great joy mixed in with the sadness that the loss brings.

"Baseball draws people together. In 2006 when Marco Scutaro hit a double down the line during the playoffs, strangers are hugging strangers. Grown men are just bawling their eyes out," Athletics super-fan MacNeil said, recalling one of his favorite baseball moments, as we lamented another forgettable playoff exit. In times that find diehard fans grappling for answers to postseason disaster, stepping back in time to recall the good times, such as Scutaro's game-winning knock a decade earlier, has a therapeutic quality. "It brings out all kinds of emotions. Baseball does that and when you're with all of your friends and you can just let loose, no one is going to judge you if you shed a tear when the season comes to a close."

We shed a tear, go our separate ways and then turn our attention to the start of a new season with renewed hope and the possibility that we will again feel everything that makes us human in the first place. Fandom gives some purpose. It gives others a chance to separate from the pressures of everyday life. But most of all, being a fan provides an instant community and with that community, we wait. We wait for the improbable; we wait for the moment of pure joy, euphoria – whatever you want to call it. The brain demands it and our psyche needs it. Diehard fans take that 50/50 chance because every now and then, the coin flip turns up in our favor, and we know that the time, money, energy, sacrifices, and passion were all worth the trouble.

BIBLIOGRAPHY

Card, David and Gordon B. Dahl. (March 2011). "Family Violence and Football: The Effect of Unexpected Emotional Cues on Violent Behavior." *Quarterly Journal of Economics.*

Espinoza, Alex. The A's Banjo Man is also a propeller hat entrepreneur. MLB.com, June 27, 2013, <http://m. mlb.com/cutfour/2013/06/27/51983800/ the-as-banjo-man-is-also-a-propeller-hat-entre-preneur>.

Falls, Joe. *Detroit Free Press*, October 11, 1968.

Kloner, Robert and Scott MacDonald. (June 15, 2009). Comparison of total and cardiovascular death rates in the same city during a losing versus winning Super Bowl championship. *American Journal of Cardiology.*

Nightengale, Bob. Owner calls dwindling crowds 'depressing'. USAToday.com, September 18, 2013, <http:// www.usatoday.com/story/sports/mlb/2013/09/ 17/dwindling-crowds-puzzling-for-contending-athletics-indians-rays/2829543/>.

Schwartz, Bryan, Robert Kloner, and Scott MacDonald. (November 2, 2013). Super Bowl outcome's association with cardiovascular death. *Clinical Research in Cardiology*.

Wann, D. L. (1995). Preliminary validation of the Sport Fan Motivation Scale. *Journal of Sport & Social Issues, 19*, 377-396.

Wann, D. L., M. P. Schrader, and A. M. Wilson. (1999). Sport fan motivation: Questionnaire validation, comparisons by sport, and relationship to athletic motivation. *Journal of Sport Behavior, 22*, 114-139.

ACKNOWLEDGMENTS

This book, a labor of love, would not have been possible if not for the gracious contributions of dozens of people to whom I am indebted. First and foremost, I would like to thank my wife Leah for her endless support, encouragement, editing expertise, and thoughtful feedback throughout the process of writing what you hold in your hand. I am thankful for my mother and stepfather, Dana and Robert, who allowed my burgeoning sports obsession to grow and evolve as a child – and who in many cases enjoyed the keystone moments right along with me. Jeff, Beth, and Jane, thank you for your encouragement and positivity throughout the writing process. To Olivia, my little baseball buddy. Thank you for sharing so many incredible memories with me at the ballpark. Watching you grow up with the game of baseball has been a thrill for me. May, my littlest lady of all, I look forward to our baseball adventures to come. Should you and your big sister choose to be fans as you both grow older, I hope sport brings you all of the joy it has provided for your daddy.

I'm appreciative of the many teachers and advisors I have had through the years, especially Dr. Michael Bishop at Baylor University. Thank you for your guidance and coaching. I offer thanks as well to the incredibly talented mentors in my professional life that challenged me to continue to refine the craft of writing, especially

Patricia Hallock, Laura Springer, Renee Wilson, and Tina Ruggiero. Special thanks to Len Bardsley, the late, great Arnold Ropeik, and Zack Hill for their mentorship and professional guidance in my early years as a writer.

Thank you to Josh Pahigian for his beautifully written foreword. I rely on Josh's book, *The Ultimate Baseball Road Trip*, for my own annual baseball travels and I'm humbled that he thought enough of my writing and the stories in Diehards to contribute his own tale of fandom.

As you read *Diehards*, you will stumble upon dozens of people who were kind enough to share their perspectives and stories with a first-time author trying to navigate his way from a blank page to a published book. I'm thankful that each took an interest in this project and in me as a writer. The encouragement that each shared with me along the way meant a great deal at every stage.

I offer thanks and appreciation to Father Jim Greanias for sharing his earliest Cubs memories and for setting the tone for this book with his keen insights on faith and fandom. Greanias was my first interview and it was through our conversation that I discovered I might have what it takes to see this project through to the end.

Thanks to Dr. Samuel Sommers for sharing his thoughts on fan psychology in a manner that made it easy for me to understand. I'm hopeful that readers will enjoy Sam's quick wit and lively personality as much as I did when we spoke.

Dr. Gabriel Torres provided me with so much more than an education in human nature and fandom. I also gained a great deal of appreciation for Torres' field, which brings new meaning to the phrase "hands-on learning."

I am humbled to have made the acquaintance of the great Dr. Daniel Wann, a leading expert in sports fan psychology and, like many others mentioned in these notes, a great fan of sports in his own right. Thank you for imparting your insights into the fan psyche.

While writing this book, I was extraordinarily fortunate that when I emailed Dr. Sandi Chapman and Dr. Leslie-Beth Wish for information about the impact of fandom on the brain they both wrote back. And when they did, both provided unique and thoughtful insights.

Jonathan Alpert provided a wealth of knowledge about counteracting the negative impacts sports obsession can have on family life. He was also one of my earliest advocates and I'm grateful for the time and energy he put into teaching me about the publishing process and introducing me to agents.

I met Bob Kendrick while on a ballpark road trip in Kansas City and his vivid stories about baseball's forgotten superstars – some of which I've included in these pages – captured my imagination and inspired me to learn more about the great Negro Leagues of a bygone era. Thank you for spending time with me and for what is always a great conversation about this beautiful game we both love so much.

Thank you to Dr. Bryan Schwartz for providing context about his own research and that of his peer Dr. Robert Kloner. I'm also grateful to Dr. Schwartz for introducing me to the work of Dr. David Card who was gracious with his time while describing his study on domestic violence and NFL fandom.

I enjoyed a lovely lunch at Charlie Gitto's Restaurant with Bill Rogers, where through his stories and overview of the great Historical Society over which he presides, I became an instant fan of the long-gone St. Louis Browns. Thank you to Emmett McAuliffe as well for offering a romantic, poetic view of Browns history.

To my fellow diehards John Ricard, Will "Right Field Will" MacNeil, and the Mayor of NatsTown Tripp

Whitbeck, thank you for sharing your stories with me. Your passion and enthusiasm for the teams you love were evident when we spoke, and I look forward to the next time we're able to kick back and talk baseball. Will, I'll see you in section 149!

Thanks to Dr. Robert Silverman for providing thoughtful perspectives on the difficult and complex topic of post-game riots.

Megan Laslocky taught me about love and heartbreak and while she was probably unsure how she, a non-fan, might fit into a book about sports, hopefully it makes more sense now.

Immense thanks to the incomparable John Thorn whose knowledge about the sport of baseball knows no bounds and whose enthusiasm as a fan is second to none.

To the friends and family members with whom I've shared countless hours talking about baseball in those hard plastic seats, especially Eric Leen, Steven Cooper, Nick Fritz-Codling, Nick Cifuentes, Michael Altfest, and Greg Cheng. I'm grateful for our shared passion and friendship.

Special thanks to Dennis Agatep for capturing the beautiful cover image used for *Diehards* and for the incredible portfolio of photos you left me with after a fun shoot at the ballpark.

I would like to thank Sherri Rowe and the good people at Rowe Publishing for giving me the opportunity to make the *Diehards* dream a reality. Thank you for shepherding me through the publishing process and for your dedication to making this book a success.

To the reader, I thank you for choosing this book and I hope you find yourself just a little bit closer to understanding why sports fans care so much about games.

On October 10, 2012, I experienced a sensation unlike any other that I've felt while watching sports. As I left the

O.co Coliseum after a euphoric finish by the Athletics, I wished I could bottle up the feelings and emotions that I felt that evening. This book is the closest I've come to doing that, and it's also a project that never would have happened had it not been for a first-pitch walk-off bleeder off the bat of Coco Crisp. So, with all of that set-up out of the way, a special thank you to Coco Crisp for creating the moment that served as my inspiration for this book.

CHIP SCARINZI is an award-winning communications executive by trade and a dyed-in-the-wool baseball fan at heart. A lifelong Philadelphia sports fan, he lives with his wife and two young daughters in the shadow of the O.co Coliseum in nearby Alameda, Calif. *Diehards* is the manifestation of his own passion for sports and a desire to understand why he and his tribe care so much about games. He is an Athletics season ticket holder, member of the Society for American Baseball Research (SABR) and spends most of his free time at the ballpark.

CPSIA information can be obtained at www.ICGtesting.com
Printed in the USA
BVOW04s0949290716

457186BV00003B/22/P